Praise for *Digi[tal]*

'I always wanted to capture the key learning points in Petra Velzeboer's presentations – now she has done it for me! This book is a timely and thought-provoking guide for anyone looking to take control of their relationship with technology. Petra draws on her expertise in mental health to address one of today's most urgent challenges: how technology shapes our lives, our minds and our relationships. With a clear and relatable style, she doesn't shy away from the tough questions, inviting readers to reflect deeply on their tech habits and take action to foster healthier, more meaningful connections. Something needed now more than ever.' ED KIRWAN, FOUNDER AND CEO, EMPATHY STUDIOS

'Given that a third of our lives are experienced through a screen, there is nothing more important than learning how to configure technology to serve us, rather than the other way around. It isn't going anywhere, so we *have* to work out how to make it work for us. Petra Velzeboer helps us get there.' RYAN HOPKINS, CHIEF IMPACT OFFICER, JAAQ AT WORK, AND AUTHOR OF *52 WEEKS OF WELLBEING*

'Finally, a book on digital wellbeing that is real, thoughtful and uplifting. The book turns a sensational topic into sensible learning. Petra Velzeboer is a masterful storyteller. She paints the landscape of digitalization in societies and then shows how and why many of us are hooked to our devices – then outlines a credible path to emotional wellbeing through richer human connections, better boundaries, and going from staring at our devices to embracing one another.

'I felt so moved and reassured after reading *Digital Wellbeing*. You will, too.' ARDESHIR MEHRAN, PSYCHOLOGIST, AUTHOR, PEAK PERFORMANCE SPEAKER

'So many of us have unwittingly become slaves to our devices. *Digital Wellbeing* not only explains the problem of digital addiction, but most importantly provides practical guidance on how to break free.' ED CROSSE, PARTNER, SIMMONS & SIMMONS LLP

'In a world where the challenges of our relationship with technology, and its potential impacts on wellbeing are ever-present, Petra Velzeboer is the ideal person to shine a light on these dangers and guide us to solutions to improve our mental health and digital wellbeing.' TODD HOPWOOD, GOVERNANCE TOP 100 FINALIST 2020–2024, AND DIRECTOR, LOCAL GOVERNMENT PROFESSIONALS AUSTRALIA

'Captures the most important issues of our time, debunking myths and giving us practical ways we can practice good mental health in work and life, and co-exist with the inevitable ubiquitous nature of technology.' NILEMA BHAKTA-JONES, MULTI-AWARD WINNING EXECUTIVE AND FOUNDER OF COURAGEOUS LEADERS

'Petra Velzeboer is one of the leading voices in this space, and rightly so. As the most popular and impactful speaker at the Make Work Better Conference 2024, it comes as no surprise that her latest book is a masterclass in reclaiming control in a world that demands so much of our attention. She blends actionable advice with powerful insights, guiding readers toward clarity, balance, and resilience. A must-read for anyone striving to thrive in both work and life.' PAUL DEVOY, CEO, INVESTORS IN PEOPLE

Digital Wellbeing

*Recharge your focus and
reboot your life*

Petra Velzeboer

Publisher's note
Every possible effort has been made to ensure that the information contained in this book is accurate at the time of going to press, and the publishers and author cannot accept responsibility for any errors or omissions, however caused. No responsibility for loss or damage occasioned to any person acting, or refraining from action, as a result of the material in this publication can be accepted by the editor, the publisher or the author.

First published in Great Britain and the United States in 2025 by Kogan Page Limited

All rights reserved. No part of this publication may be reproduced, stored or transmitted by any means without prior written permission from Kogan Page, except as permitted under applicable copyright laws.

Kogan Page
Kogan Page Ltd, 2nd Floor, 45 Gee Street, London EC1V 3RS, United Kingdom
Kogan Page Inc, 8 W 38th Street, Suite 90, New York, NY 10018, USA
www.koganpage.com

EU Representative (GPSR)
Authorised Rep Compliance Ltd, Ground Floor, 71 Lower Baggot Street, Dublin D02 P593, Ireland
www.arccompliance.com

Kogan Page books are printed on paper from sustainable forests.

© Petra Velzeboer, 2025

The moral rights of the author have been asserted.

ISBNs
Hardback   978 1 3986 1754 4
Paperback   978 1 3986 1753 7
Ebook   978 1 3986 1757 5

British Library Cataloguing-in-Publication Data
A CIP record for this book is available from the British Library.

Library of Congress Control Number
2024050212

Typeset by Integra Software Services, Pondicherry
Print production managed by Jellyfish
Printed and bound by CPI Group (UK) Ltd, Croydon CR0 4YY

Contents

Introduction 1

1 Always on: The digital grind 17

Smartphones: a brief history and impact 18
How to know if you're stuck in the digital grind 22
Fear of technology 26
How do we pinpoint the problem? 27
Is tech really addictive? 28
Compulsion or addiction? 30
What is your digital grind? 34

2 The psychology of digital wellbeing 37

Potential and why it matters 37
What stops us reaching potential: being stuck in survival mode 39
What does all this have to do with technology? 41
Belonging and negativity bias 41
Braving the messy middle and taking ownership of our lives 43
Being seen: developing early attachments 44
What are attachment styles? 45
Burnout, crash points and danger zones 50
Are we responsible for changing our relationship to technology or is it a bigger issue? 53
Summary 55

3 Comfortably numb: Overcoming digital malaise 57
   Symptoms of digital malaise 58
   How our devices are keeping us stuck 60
   To challenge digital malaise, we must embrace our humanity 61
   How our earliest experiences shape us 61
   Making life easier or better? 63
   Getting the foundations right 66
   The commoditization of emotion 69
   How to challenge digital malaise 73
   Summary 75

4 Set up to fail? How the machine holds us back 77
   What cults can teach us about the machine 79
   Is digital detox the solution? 80
   Cults and the need to belong 82
   Wellbeing hacks: selling solutions to man-made problems 84
   Stress and misinformation 87
   Groupthink 88
   Groupthink and how we relate to others 90
   Artificial intelligence 91
   AI therapies and support 93
   Summary 95

5 Fighting loneliness and finding humanity 97
   You are not alone 99
   Quantum energy and remote work 101
   How loneliness shapes us 104
   Connection: a skill to develop 105

Stigma and taboo 107
How we can take responsibility for our wellbeing 109
How to boost humanity 111
Assess your digital and wellbeing practices – do you feel lonely or connected? 113
A lonely society and how to create change 118

6 How to thrive in the digital world 121
What does good look like? Wellbeing and mental health 122
What does good look like? Work and focus 123
Setting intentions 124
How to ask for feedback 129
Grassroots solutions 130
So how do we thrive in a digital age? 132
Building community 137
Can you trust your feelings? 141
Building safe spaces 142
Summary 144

7 Create your tech boundaries 147
Assess your ability to set boundaries 147
Types of boundaries 148
How do you know you need a boundary? 149
How to create a vision for your life 150
The digital detox 155

8 Find your focus and reclaim your joy 163
How to cultivate joy 164
What's all the fuss about focus? 171

A little tough love – snowflakes, resilience and thriving 173
The Five Regrets of the Dying 175
Progress, not perfection 176
Action steps 179

Conclusion 181

References 187
Index 195

Introduction

If you've picked up this book, you're probably curious and aware of the toll that technology is taking on your life – and you want to know if there's a different way to live.

Perhaps you can't quite figure out why your body and mind are so tired, why your relationships feel fraught or your joy has diminished over the years, and you wonder if maybe there's a simple hack that can help you recharge your focus and reboot your life.

You've come to the right place.

What if I told you that how you're feeling isn't just your fault? That you're a product of your environment in a world that is competing for your attention and the constant pull in every direction is impacting how you feel?

This is a huge topic of course and as I sit at a blank page, I contemplate the vastness of it and the way that I might uniquely tackle it. There's AI of course and the nervousness we have about how this will change our lives, infinity scrolling on social media, our always-on culture, lack of focus and hard-to-reach work-life balance. We're impacted by distraction, consumerism, comparing, addiction and poor mental health. Many of us are frazzled at the pace of change, burnt out, stressed out, navigating overwhelm at the state of the world, the state of our young people and simply don't know how to switch off as we hustle the side-hustle and decry being always on.

I also see the countless benefits the digital world brings – like free video calls to anywhere in the world, being able to work remotely, connecting with our tribes globally and many grassroots projects impacting the world for good.

Is technology the problem?

From where I'm sitting, technology is neither good nor evil. My main aim for this book is to help you press pause on all your distractions and help you think for yourself. To weigh up the evidence of technology on your wellbeing yes, but, most importantly, to weigh up how you feel on the inside. This book is a chance to reflect on you – your relationship to technology, your relationships in general, your life, your physical and mental health – and ask yourself some powerful questions, such as:

- Am I using technology to create a more efficient life – one that creates space for joy?

- Is technology the gateway to deeper connection with my people?
- Does my digital world boost my wellbeing or hinder it?
- Am I using technology intentionally or is it using me?

If you, like me, sometimes feel frazzled or addicted to technology you may sometimes dream of just walking away, living off-grid and finding a simpler life – the fantasy of rolling fields, music and peace.

If only we could apply the logic of addicts to other substances to the digital landscape. As someone who has struggled with alcohol addiction, the solution has always been simple – never drink again. Imagine if those of us at risk of tech addiction could simply choose not to engage with screens and instead opt for a paper map, a brick phone and regular old alarm clock.

But that feels impossible in today's world, right?

All aspects of the world are now geared towards technology – from work to community to dating, travelling, banking, socializing and leisure, basically everything you can think of from telling the time to finding your way to staying cool and connected are all hotwired in this portable device you take everywhere. Going digitally teetotal would mean that you become an outcast, living off-grid and completely disconnected from modern society. You might be viewed by others as a suspicious luddite and it's likely it would be nearly impossible for you to keep a job, manage your finances, pay your bills or travel freely.

At the other extreme, there is the privileged digital detoxer who has a high-stress job but finds it easy to afford to spend a few weeks each year at expensive retreats where everything is catered to and their phone is strategically locked in a safe while they meditate and find their zen – all while their assistant is efficiently managing their lives so that they can reintegrate seamlessly into busy modern society refreshed and without skipping a beat. This feels out of reach for many of us too.

The trouble is, for all the good of a digital detox acting as a glorious reset, it's only a matter of time before any of us would slowly slip back into the cycle of distracted attention – forgetting to be present and connected – eventually forcing us to once again try to figure out a tech rehab or other creative solution to manage a wired brain and continue to function in a burnt-out and mentally risky world.

How does your relationship to technology feel?

In November 2023, I ran a rudimentary poll on LinkedIn and asked, 'Does your relationship to your phone negatively impact your mental health?' and out of 250 respondents, 69 per cent said yes and 31 per cent said no – but the comments were interesting. A handful of people told me that their relationship to their phone had boosted their mental health in some way, including saying things like:

> Yes, it does (affect my mental health). Net positive impact though, not negative. It allows me to keep in touch with people I care about, learn about fascinating topics, discover new music, watch things that make me laugh… the list goes on.

> I would say it complements it as a matter of fact. I think of it as all relative based on what the intentions are when utilizing such technologies.

A recent YouGov study (2024), spanning a period of five years and with ages ranging from 18–65, asked the question: 'In general, do you think that social media has a broadly positive or broadly negative effect on your mental health?' While the findings fluctuated slightly year on year, on average 33 per cent felt there was a negative impact on their mental health, with 15 per cent stating a broadly positive impact.

So, my intention with this book is not to decry technology but to embrace it. Yes, sometimes we can navigate a healthy relationship with technology just as the alcoholic might stick to just one glass of wine, but we can also find ourselves on the precipice of a battle for our own wellbeing. This battle is where I want to focus.

Focusing on digital wellbeing is a key step to achieving your goals and improving your life; that business you want to build, those relationships that are struggling, the burnout you want to overcome, the general malaise and overwhelm of modern life – digital wellbeing holds the key to moving you in the right direction.

This book is for anyone who, like me, has thrown their phone across the room fed up with its hold on them. It is for anyone who has felt like technology has become a third person in their relationship. This book is for anyone who is trying to build a good life but loses hours to social media or other digital distractions. It's for the people who say they don't have time to invest in themselves, their aspirations or relationships and yet their phone regularly reminds them of the hours spent daily on their device, taking them away from their true north.

This book is for anyone who wants an open conversation about how we can use technology for good while also addressing the challenges and struggles. It's easy to feel weak-willed, foolish or depressed when struggling to overcome these issues and yet this is a collective and societal issue that we should be navigating together.

This book is also for you if you are displaying a variety of symptoms but just can't put your finger on what's wrong. You may be experiencing depression, anxiety or burnout. You might be medicating, in therapy or focusing on physical or mental symptoms while ignoring environmental factors that are affecting you to the core – you may simply not know where to start. So let's start together.

Why this topic matters to me

Mental health at work is a topic close to my heart and one that I've tackled in depth in my first book *Begin with You* (2023). In that book, I talk extensively about mental health, burnout, creating internal change in the workplace and critically assessing your own life, what you want and how to think differently to enable you to get there. I talk about internal activism, groupthink and the mental health agenda globally.

This book is personal because it affects me, my kids and the organizations I work with globally. I use my expertise as a psychotherapist and coach who has worked with hundreds of individuals to help them create fulfilling lives, as a mental health and wellbeing consultant who has worked with countless international teams, as a youth counsellor and parent of teenagers who has seen the shift in one generation from play and imagination to hyperconnection and worsening mental health statistics – and mostly, as a curious addict who has felt the negatives of tech addiction (or technostress as it's called today) but also the immense positives of being able to build a fully remote and flexible team as well as stay connected with friends and family globally.

I also grew up in a cult. Being born into this lifestyle highlights how the most extreme conditions can become normalized if you don't know how to question them. In the same way our world of attention, competition and often toxic environments can become so normal that we simply blame ourselves when we experience the negative symptoms of these environments. It must be our fault that we're burnt out or physically and mentally unwell because we live in a cult of busy, where it's normalized to be frazzled and always on, never questioning what's behind the scenes creating the problem while then selling us the solution.

Blame the individual if they are not healthy within a system that is sick. Gaslight the person who is doubting the environment by saying, well maybe you're just not cut out for this, you're no longer a culture fit, you should probably see a professional, sort out your brain and when you're well, come back and act like everything is normal – our version of normal. Growing up in a cult which was the only world I knew meant it took decades to figure out that the way I was feeling was not my fault, but instead it was because I was a product of my environment, the slow crushing weight of shame and secrecy impacting my mental health – not to be cured by a three-step Instagram hack but rather a Pandora's box issue that would take time, radical honesty and bravery to slowly unpick, question and totally change.

So my intention with this book is to bring the topic of technostress and tech addiction into the light so we can set useful and workable intentions to boost our focus and create happier lives.

Let's get honest together about what's really going on. What we're feeling, how we're colluding in the problem, the emotions we're avoiding and how we're suffering behind the scenes so that together we can develop the skills and resilience necessary to thrive in a fast-paced digital world.

What is digital wellbeing?

First, let's get down to basics and see if we can start with a shared understanding about what digital wellbeing is. What are we even working towards and how will we know when we get there?

Digital wellbeing is a new and evolving concept, and its definition will vary depending on personal perspectives as well as cultural contexts. Dr Paul Marsden (2020) summarized 34 different answers to the question 'What is digital wellbeing?' from the likes of Google and experts globally and came up with this definition: 'digital wellbeing is a state of personal wellbeing experienced through the healthy use of digital technology'. Of course, digital wellbeing is also a Google program, an Android app, a TikTok feature, a BBC feature and the name of the site that collated this information.

So, it seems to be both personal and subjective. Great. No wonder we're confused. In order to figure out what 'good' digital wellbeing looks like, let's break it down by considering the areas of our lives that have potential impacts on our general health, happiness and fulfilment. In a world of wearable tech, productivity hacks and hybrid work, let's begin by assessing where we're at personally through the lens of what we do and how we feel.

Here are four key areas we can start with to help us assess how we're feeling.

Physical health

Begin by assessing your physical health. Is your digital usage such as screen time affecting things like sleep or does your sedentary lifestyle filled with ease and efficiency negatively impact heart health, posture, weight and overall physical wellbeing? How does your body feel each day? Do you know how to listen to what your body is telling you? Your body is a wealth of information about your environment. Just like a plant will thrive in great soil and under great conditions, is your body thriving in its environment or slowly withering away?

Mental health

Do you spiral into addictions such as endless scrolling, negative comparing or envy of others, shopping beyond your financial means and avoiding tasks that need focus? Does pornography use impact your relationships or do you feel like you sometimes have no control over the time spent aimlessly distracted?

Have you ever set boundaries around your tech use only to spiral into a state of dejection, frustrated that you're back in the cycle you tried to move away from? Are you anxious, overwhelmed, strung out or burnt out?

Real and meaningful connection

In some ways we are more connected than ever before, but are these connections authentic or are we interacting through masks and gathering fake information that is making us more polarized?

Do we have conversations that are meaningful and go beyond the surface interactions or are we hiding behind pleasantries, experiencing more isolation and loneliness than ever before?

Cognitive function and focus

Do you understand how your data is used, how algorithms present information to you, how notifications can fire up your survival impulses and how information overload can leave you paralysed and unable to take action?

Are we procrastinating or are we actually in a state of physiological freeze; fear and overwhelm stuck in our nervous systems making it impossible to do anything other than firefight? This may feel like productivity in the short term but over time leads to crash-points, brain fog and burnout as we switch tasks and impede productivity rather than boost it.

Throughout this book I will go into these areas in depth to help you find the solutions that are right for you.

Why mental health and addiction in a topic about digital health?

The two definitions that most stand out to me, as they align with the overall World Health Organization definition of Mental Health, are:

> A state of satisfaction that people achieve when digital technology supports their intentions – *Google Toolkit for Developers*

and

> The conscious use of technology which enables individuals and communities to reach their potential – *Georgie Powell, digital wellbeing and responsible technology expert*

The definition of mental health according to the World Health Organization (2022) includes the phrase 'a state of wellbeing… where an individual can achieve their potential… can work productively and fruitfully and is able to make a contribution to their community'.

So the question to help you assess your digital health might be, is your relationship to technology boosting your ability to achieve potential and work productively through boosting your physical health, community and sense of fulfilment or is it doing the opposite?

You may wonder if the word addiction actually applies to you, so I'll touch on the difference between compulsions and addictions, and help identify those of us who are at greater risk of harm from digital technologies and what we can do to keep ourselves in check, walking the tightrope of digital usage through the tough times in life as well as the good times – and as ever, using radical honesty and accountability to enable us to do so.

The environments making us sick: how to challenge the system

Many tech companies are fighting for our attention and working tirelessly to keep us on their platforms, which means there's only so much each of us as individuals can do to manage things without questioning the system at large, as done so eloquently by Johann Hari in his book *Stolen Focus* (2023). His findings include his journey and some tactics of course (silencing notifications, taking breaks, etc); however, he challenges us to join the movements that are working to change the system to better protect our digital health, privacy and the addictive nature they are working hard to achieve. He notes: 'Systemic problems require systemic solutions. We have to take individual responsibility for this problem for sure, but at the same time, together we have to take collective responsibility for dealing with these deeper factors.'

So while I want to add to the literature out there in order to give you a grounding in tools, tactics, mindsets and actions, it's worth remembering what we're up against – a system that is set up to create the problems and then manufacture the apps and hacks to help us handle the problems that they have created.

Our experiences and conclusions will be subjective and personal and my aim in this book is to ask fundamental questions that will enable you to come to your own conclusions.

Limitations

It's also worth stating the limitations of this book. The world is full of digital poverty – vast inequalities in the world when it comes to digital opportunity, leading to a deficiency of digital skills and access. This can have hugely negative consequences, including poorer health outcomes, increased loneliness and isolation and less access to jobs and opportunities.

For the sake of this short book my aim is to focus on those of us with access and skills for digital engagement who are feeling burnt out, overwhelmed or addicted and wanting to reboot our focus in order to enhance our wellbeing and joy in life. You may be wondering about boundaries in a modern age, achieving your goals in a world of distraction and connecting more deeply to others to stave off loneliness and poor mental health.

What to expect in this book

I will ask what I believe are fundamental questions that can help you shape your relationship to technology and thereby boost your overall wellbeing, including:

- If technology is set up to be addictive, what can we regular people do to avoid falling into the addiction trap –

and what, if anything, can those of us who are already addicts do to manage the middle road and use technology for good?
- In a world of debilitating mental health and poor wellbeing, what part does technology play and how can we get radically honest about what we can do to boost our own wellbeing and that of our teams and families in a rapidly changing world?
- And finally, if technology is meant to make us more hyperconnected, why are so many of us feeling lonely and out of practice in curating true connection and belonging – and crucially, what can we do to feel better about how we work, love and connect?

We'll start with the experience of being always on, outlining the digital grind and feeling of overwhelm many of us are facing. Many of us are holding our hands up in despair as we look around and think there's nothing we can do about all this change and so we keep our heads firmly in the sand, just focusing on our immediate circumstances, perhaps complaining about how it's all gone wrong but feeling too tired to do anything about it.

Given my background as a psychotherapist and mental health expert I'll outline the psychology of digital wellbeing and what all this change is doing to our brain, relationships and workplaces, all the while offering questions to prompt your thinking about your own life and what you may need to do to adjust your relationship to technology in order to thrive alongside this fast pace of change.

More and more I see people using technology to numb their feelings or avoid tricky things like eye contact, conversation in real life (IRL) or engaging with their community, atrophying the skills necessary to feel seen and valued in order to boost mental health in a more isolating world.

I'll touch on the massive technological shifts we are facing such as how quickly artificial intelligence is changing things and the fears and hopes this brings to society. More than ever we need to keep our wits about us to check our influences, challenge fake news and make decisions on our own body and soul rather than succumb to the pressures, opinions and information all around us.

I'll touch on addiction and those of us for whom simple structures like balance and boundaries don't seem to work, providing clues as to why this occurs and bring into the light the discussions so that it can't pull us down in shame and secrecy.

We'll go deep into loneliness and crucially the tactics that can enable you to live a full and rich life even in urban cities where connection is transient and can feel like an uphill struggle.

While I use story and offer practical solutions throughout the book, in the final chapters I will offer insights, tools and questions to help you assess your relationship to technology and help you zoom out on your life, what matters to you most and the sometimes brave, necessary steps that will enable you to look back on your life with joy and peace.

Using my personal experience as a parent, mental health expert and addict, I invite you on a journey to assess where you're at personally when it comes to your digital health and will offer tools and ideas to enable radical honesty so you can wake up to your personal relationship to technology. We can collectively take radical responsibility for the world we are in, ensuring technology acts as the great enabler it has the potential to be – one that can evolve our workplaces, boost efficiency and create space for meaningful connection and building a life we really want.

Let's reboot our lives and recharge our focus!

CHAPTER ONE

Always on: The digital grind

This chapter title already sounds depressing.

I'm pretty sure you know what I mean and can relate when I say always on. Maybe you've even let out a sigh, thinking, 'Right?! It's like I'm ALWAYS ON, there's no PEACE, I wish I could just be left alone and be able to breathe for FIVE minutes!' Or perhaps a less intense version of that sentiment. While there are plenty of benefits and exciting developments that add perks to our lives in this digital age, let's have a moment to recognize the challenge that is in front of us.

If you're old enough, like me, you might remember an internet-free age. Nostalgically, people who remember may say things like 'back in my day we just got on with it and entertained ourselves. Yes, we were bored but that's when we made things, invented situations and developed ideas.' While there are benefits to the technological age, it's interesting to note that according to psychologists, free play without technology supports childhood development, including teaching life skills such as adaptability, resilience, self-reliance and creative thinking as well as interpersonal skills to help manage early conflicts and get used to living and working in communities.

As Johann Hari puts it in his book *Stolen Focus: Why you can't pay attention* (2023):

> We aren't just facing a crisis of lost focus – we are facing a crisis of lost mind-wandering... without mind-wandering we find it harder to make sense of the world... and we become even more vulnerable to the next distraction that comes along.

So, if boosting our wellbeing is about reaching our potential and making a contribution to our communities, is our inability to mind-wander and keep our attention on any one thing for long negatively impacting the skills that we need to enable us to deliver on this ideal? I say skills because while our environment, culture and socialization massively impact our wellbeing, there are skills that can be developed to put us in a position to combat the negatives of technology while utilizing tech to enable greater potential and connection.

Smartphones: a brief history and impact

While computers have been in the picture as far back as 1937, when it comes to focus and attention, it's the rapid pace of change since the smartphone that has really impacted our attention and wellbeing.

The first smartphone was released in 1992 and has only really been in everyone's pockets since the 2000s, with the first iPhone being released in 2007, the Android in 2008 and phones emerging in significant markets from 2010. Which means that if you're in your 40s or older, most of your adult life you have lived without access to everything imaginable in your very pocket, and instead had to read maps, tell the time, read road signs, work with actual humans and perhaps even use a calendar to map out your life – and certainly at times stare into the middle distance or stand in a long queue, bored!

My kids were born in 2003 and 2006 and already the space of those three years between them (both technically Gen Z) is a vastly different relationship to technology. My older son is not a TikTok native and has different uses for technology than my younger daughter, whose attention span already seems to have shrunk and easily uses AI platforms for research, talks to Siri like a friend and has no issue being tracked on Snapchat Maps where all friends are seen at all times (unless activating what's known as 'ghost mode' to not be seen).

Even before the Covid-19 pandemic in 2020 the world was escalating in speed and efficiency at such pace that our mental health was taking a hit at having to adapt so quickly all of the time – from learning new technologies and communication strategies, to globalization, job insecurities and needing to develop new skills more quickly to stay relevant.

While there are pros and cons to technology and I want to be balanced in my views, watching the 2020 documentary

The Social Dilemma on Netflix made me want to burn all smartphones everywhere due to the striking statistics correlating smartphone usage and poor mental health (Orlowski, Coombe and Curtis, 2020).

The most striking evidence in the documentary has to do with our young people. Jonathan Haidt PhD, social psychologist and author of books such as *The Anxious Generation* (2024) quotes studies including US hospital admissions for older girls aged 15–19 and preteens aged 10–14, noting that incidents of self-harm were pretty stable and then went way up. 'There has been a gigantic increase in depression and anxiety for American teenagers which began right around 2011 to 2013,' he states, 'It's up 62 per cent for older girls. It's up 189 per cent for preteen girls – that's nearly triple!'

He goes on to outline a similar uptick in suicides taken from data from the US Center for Disease Control and Prevention, with the 'same pattern, with suicide up by 70 per cent comparable to the first decade of the century and preteen girls up by 151 per cent!' The graph then very clearly aligns this uptick in horrific events with the advent of social media in a pocket device from 2009. My heart just breaks as I read through these statistics again, knowing how many families have been shattered by this reality.

The Social Dilemma documentary goes on to highlight further challenges including less privacy, data mining, misinformation and algorithms narrowing people's viewpoints, with incidents such as the 2016 US election being hotly debated as being influenced by Facebook algorithms.

When we think of ethics and how we are managing these negative impacts connected to social platforms, my research brings me to a fascinating platform of honest research and debate. The Center for Humane Technology (2021), co-founded by the American technology ethicist Tristan Harris, outlines the extensive risk areas that should have better safety measures and offers resources and ideas for managing our attention and wellbeing.

Tristan's journey started in 2013, when he was a Google Design Ethicist who created a viral presentation called 'A Call to Minimize Distraction and Respect Users' Attention', which was followed by two TED Talks that sparked the Time Well Spent movement and acted as groundwork for the founding of The Center for Humane Technology.

A brief overview of some of the risks, which I'm sure you could add to, includes:

- New generations: Our young people face unprecedented physical, mental and social challenges exacerbated by fast-changing tech, isolation and comparing on a global scale.
- Attention and mental health: Technology is competing for our attention, weakening our memory and driving addiction, loneliness and depression.
- Misinformation: Synthetic media, sensationalism and coordinated bots are destroying our information ecosystem, making it hard to know what is true in a world of fake news.
- Politics and clickbait: Maximizing engagement often amplifies outrage, deepens divisions and reduces empathy, which is eroding shared consensus.
- Privacy: Our data is exploited by an industry that extracts our attention, shapes our thoughts and behaviours and makes us vulnerable to risks – all for profit.

No wonder we're always on and experiencing the digital grind – it's the way the system is set up!

How to know if you're stuck in the digital grind

So, what is it about this digital world, then, that has so many of us feeling burnt out, exhausted, overwhelmed and disconnected? What in fact is a digital grind?

The dictionary definition of grind (Dictionary.com, nd) has many angles but here's a few it might be useful to reflect on:

- to wear, smoothe or sharpen by abrasion or friction
- to oppress, torment or crush
- to perform a monotonous task repeatedly in order to advance a character to a higher level or rank (in a video game)

With these varied definitions in mind, let's start by reflecting on how we feel, something we often don't take the time to do in our always-on culture. Ask yourself how you feel at work, during time off, relaxation and connection. It's useful to get right back to basics. How are you sleeping? Do you feel rested and resourced after a weekend or vacation? Do you feel like your connections are meaningful or instead do you feel a sense of always being in a hurry, that everything is urgent and that even when you're relaxing you're doing three things at once or perhaps feeling like you're behind or missing something.

As far as I see it, there are a few key things that impact how we feel:

- **Distraction:** Doing many things at once at the expense of focusing on the things that really matter to you.
- **Comparing:** Thinking everyone else is somehow doing more or better than you in their work, side-hustles or even in their leisure time, leading to a feeling of disconnection and envy rather than community.
- **Lack of autonomy:** A feeling of being watched, leading to checking emails at all hours and staying tapped in at all times.

Distraction: do you know what matters to you

A key symptom of digital grind is being busy. I know, it doesn't quite make sense because doesn't busy mean impactful, effective or productive? Well, no, it really doesn't. Being busy can be jumping from one thing to another, constantly in a rush, feeling like everything is urgent, being in meetings and saying yes to lots of things at the expense of the great things.

We've all been there. We've rushed around all day and when we really reflect on what we've done our big tasks or the things that really matter to us are still there, staring at us on a list of to-dos. Busy-ness is often a trap. It makes us feel good about ourselves in the short term and like we fit into an always-on society but when we get older and take time to reflect, we often lament the fact that we never did the things that truly mattered to us – instead we rushed around frazzled in a constant state of alert with limited forward action.

Distractions are exasperated by pings, pop-ups and ads drawing us away from our greatness and into short-term excitement but long-term distress.

Comparing and the rise of the side-hustle

We live in an age where you can start a business from your bedroom at any age and experiment with what you love doing and make money from it quickly. How amazing is that! Having had a side-hustle myself alongside my studies and day job for years, I am an absolute advocate for using technology to build a life you love.

However, in big cities, with a cost-of-living crisis and consumerism making us feel like we always need more money and stuff, the side-hustle has almost become expected. 'You mean you only focus on a day job and that's it? You're not out scaling a startup, running a marathon or climbing Everest in your spare time? How very quaint.'

Being able to see other people's highlight reel while we eat ice cream and binge-watch Netflix has a unique effect on us. Even if we've been busy all day, rushing around doing things, by the time we crash out we can hardly enjoy it because we think we're not even doing downtime or wellbeing right. Look at us in our joggers, eating Ben & Jerry's from the tub while watching *Love Island*. What losers. Everyone else has it figured out while we don't.

This comparing to others keeps us busy playing by other people's rules rather than reflecting on what we want and stripping out distractions in order to do the things that really matter to us.

If we're running everybody else's race, it's really difficult to see our own path or have any kind of strategy for the experience we want in this one short life we are given a gift to live.

Lack of autonomy

A close friend of mine works in the United States in a job that she would describe as having zero autonomy, a feeling of being watched through the green light on Microsoft Teams, and a digital tracking of every task done with a target for each day, each week, each month of repetitive grinding work that she is assessed on at the end of each month. If she is proactive and fast, she is *rewarded* with more work and if she is slow, she's at risk of being fired, so the art really is to stay somewhere in the middle of mediocre productivity so that not too much is expected but equally she isn't noticed for slacking.

Autonomy is the right to make decisions for yourself and is crucial for our wellbeing, a feeling of having some agency over the direction of our lives.

My friend's workplace is frankly the opposite of what promoting wellbeing should look like if we're to take the WHO definition to heart – it encourages her to remain mediocre and in her lane. Do not reach your potential or give to your community; instead use all your energy to play a game of cat and mouse, in fear of being fired, leading to stress-based symptoms you can't quite quantify but will be blamed for if they limit your ability to play said game.

Work cultures coupled with comparing and fear can make us feel like we must check our emails at all hours, respond no matter what time it is, bring our laptop to the beach on holiday and check our devices every few minutes just in case, on the off chance, something important comes in right then. For many of us the difference between an endless to-do list vs what is urgent has been conflated to the point that everything feels urgent and so the grind is constant busyness, fear of missing out or the worry of being shamed for getting something wrong.

Fear of technology

Every generation in history has decried the next one – fearful of an end to morals, values or simply stating this is the way we've always done it, therefore everything else is bad. It's a frequent echo of each older and wiser generation.

When the first telephones and TVs were placed in homes, people were genuinely scared, thinking our children's brains would turn to mush. Technophobia first became a thing back in the Industrial Revolution with a group of Luddites literally rioting when automated looms came in to disrupt their ways of doing things and parliament needing to pass a law saying destruction of machines would be an offence (University of Cambridge, 2012).

Fear of progress is still with us, as we see the debates around AI and how it will destroy the workplace of the future with extreme fears around AI developing consciousness or even making humans extinct. Many of us are collectively panicking at the rise of the machines and yet feeling we have no choice but to just get on with our lives alongside technology.

When we can't predict an outcome, when we don't understand how to use new tech or when our kids speak a totally different language to us – we get nervous! We look for what's wrong and ignore the good, such as virtual reality utilized for surgeons to practise before working on humans, the speed with which organ donors can now be found, our ability to speak to a loved one and see their face on video for free, low-cost travel and how we broadly live safe and efficient lives, enabling a higher potential for self-actualization and developing our minds and creatively enhancing our environments.

How do we pinpoint the problem?

You may never have labelled digital overwhelm as a real issue, just a symptom of the modern world, with *stress* being your real issue – maybe your boss sending emails late and expecting a reply or feeling like you must work while on holiday. Whatever you think is the source, whether it's a you problem or a them problem, you may simply feel the symptoms of anxious thinking, lethargy or low mood, exhaustion, overwhelm or that nagging feeling of disconnection and loneliness even though you engage with people all the time!

Stress is not the main problem – or at least not regular stress which can actually help push us to build resilience and potential. What we're experiencing is a new type of stress, something that may be more insidious, that we haven't quite evolved fast enough to manage effectively. Stress that keeps us firmly in survival mode and holds a very real threat of leading us to compulsive or addictive behaviours that over time impact our mental health negatively. Whether you are in the camp that says it's a self-discipline and boundaries issue, a personal one to be handled or if you're in the camp that says it's a much broader, systemic issue – we are all being impacted by the fast pace of change. We are wired for connection and chase the feel-good hormone dopamine. If a hit of dopamine comes through the device in our hand or our wearables, well hey, life's pretty tough on the whole so we'll get happy wherever we can.

Long term, it's never as simple as that. We might say that chasing dopamine can become addictive.

Is tech really addictive?

A friend of mine recently challenged me about the addictive component of technology. He emphatically said it's not the fault of the devices or the technologies, it's not a systemic issue, it's simply how we use them – after all there are many settings and productivity tools that can help us use them in the right way. Just check your settings and be intentional about your usage. Sounds simple when put like that.

You may not identify with the idea of addiction or think you fall into the addiction camp. Many of you might in fact be able to manage your productivity by switching off effectively and don't see yourself scrolling mindlessly on TikTok but you might still lose hours on Netflix or emails, you might be on Facebook or eBay or gaming or a million other ways of experiencing that buzz of a problem that you can't quite put your finger on. Must be getting older, or be frazzled because you're young, or in perimenopause or just in a stressful time of your life. We can be hard on ourselves too, thinking it's just us and this is where the dark side of technology shows up – everyone else seems fine, we tell ourselves. I mean, everyone has problems, but the online versions of their lives look great, it's just me that can't seem to get this boundary thing right, achieve my goals, sleep well, sustain a relationship or feel just, well, well!

My friend is of course partly right – there are lots of productivity tools and settings that can enable us to manage our technology use. However, with a business model that is about competing for your attention, you may lack the awareness or education on the impacts of technology on your mental health and the real threats to your wellbeing; you are not given instruction on the ways to protect yourself and perhaps only begin to figure these hacks out once you're frazzled and looking for answers.

Effective digital education is key if we're going to adapt effectively together to our fast pace of change. This should start in schools, with parents and with the purchase of any new phone. It's got to infiltrate into the conversations we have at work, too, so that we stop building hospitals at the proverbial bottom of the cliff, but instead build fences at the top.

Many people simply don't know that they need a fence at all. They just follow the next thing in front of them, enjoying the fun or convenience, not realizing that they are pawns in a game of digital attention. How can people set the right settings or take responsibility for how they use technology if they don't know there's a problem to begin with?

Compulsion or addiction?

But let's go to addiction first and see whether this is really applicable to the vast majority of us or just the smaller percentage of people – like our young people whose brains are still developing or people like me who have to handle addiction to other substances by going teetotal.

Dr Ann Lembke, Medical Director of Addiction Medicine at Stanford University's School of Medicine, said in the documentary *The Social Dilemma*:

> Social media is a drug. We have a basic biological imperative to connect that directly affects the release of dopamine, there are millions of years of evolution behind that… so there is no doubt that a vehicle like social media which optimizes this connection is going to have the potential for addiction.

According to the *Merriam-Webster Dictionary*, compulsion is 'an irresistible, persistent impulse to perform an act' while an addiction is seen as a 'chronic, physiological or psychological need for a habit-forming substance, behaviour, or activity having harmful effects and typically causing symptoms (such as anxiety, irritability, tremors or nausea) upon withdrawal or abstinence.'

You may have up to this point resisted the idea of your device or technology being addictive for you. Maybe sometimes an annoying habit that sucks away time but definitely not addictive in the extreme sense of having direct harmful effects – you may even have said a version of 'well I can stop at any time, I just don't want to' and therefore decide you're not that bad and it's all, well, manageable. Let's try a little experiment to see if this is true.

Put your phone in another room, turn it off completely or go out and leave it at home – see how long it takes you to feel a phantom vibration in your pocket, for your thumb to feel like it's missing its purpose or your anxiety to surge or irritability to surface?

A lesser experiment might be turning off all notifications, deleting email apps, Instagram, the news or whatever it is that sucks your attention, making sure it takes three steps instead of one to gain access. Watch and notice how long it takes you to incessantly check anyway; taking those three steps is no barrier to your need to check email on the weekend or social channels when you just literally checked! Yes, your notifications are off as you follow the guidance to be responsible for your access and yet the compulsion is so strong that you find a way through regardless of the barriers you have placed in front of yourself.

What did you discover in doing this experiment?

This is a simple experiment but may very well offer information on the hold you didn't think your device had on you and the choices you didn't realize were partly leading your life. In his 2017 book *Irresistible: The rise of addictive technology and the business of keeping us hooked*, Adam Alter states, 'We're not quite at the point where we can talk about addiction to social networks or online data in the way we talk about addiction to drugs or alcohol, but there's little doubt that these mechanisms are designed to be as addictive as possible.'

In 2025 I would confidently say this idea has evolved and that for some, addiction to technology is killing them. This seems like a strong statement, I realize, but remember the alcoholic or addict doesn't die from addiction-related complications overnight – it's a slow stacking of stressors on the body and mind that are ignored and disregarded, that slowly, slowly, suck their very life away.

There are risk factors for being more susceptible of course and the next chapter goes into depth on the psychology of digital wellbeing; however, there's a simple little acronym that addicts use to know that the fence at the top needs some repair – HALT. Funny how the acronym works; it's a warning to pause and reflect, to notice the conditions in your life that may make you more susceptible to the negatives of compulsion or addiction in that moment. The acronym outlines the human risk factors that can make us more susceptible to avoidance or addiction, and stands for:

H – Hungry
A – Angry
L – Lonely
T – Tired

Pretty basic, right? When we're frazzled and aren't getting our basic needs for sleep, food or connection and are unable to regulate our emotions due to triggers, stress or overwhelm, we are at greater risk of grabbing whatever is in reach to give us a quick dopamine hit so we can move away from these uncomfortable feelings for just a moment.

Our digital distractions may not seem to lead to the same carnage as an addiction to drugs but there are also countless addicts hiding in plain sight, in the shadows of shame, unable to solve their struggle.

As the great Dr Brene Brown, in her extensive work on vulnerability and shame, highlights, 'Shame cannot survive being spoken, it cannot tolerate having words wrapped around it. What it craves is silence, secrecy and judgement' (Brown, 2015), and so on the topic of our digital health I want to open us up to the real conversation, to challenge shame and digital malaise so we can help each other step into the light.

This doesn't mean living off grid and never using technology. We love technology!

I get to work remotely, speak to friends globally and manage my schedule, emails and life from a device that fits in my pocket. How crazy good is that?! But I've also had to challenge the risks of the digital grind by listening to friends who call me out on my phone usage, creating space for reflection and joy, separating out work life from life life and taking the time to reflect and notice the deep-seated psychology that affects all of us. We want to belong, connect and be part of something. We are so desperate for this feeling, in fact, that we will do anything to feel it even for a moment, even if that means in the long term we die of addiction – or worse. What's worse than that, you may ask – well, I'll tell you.

What's worse is dying a slow death of mediocrity, never quite knowing what's wrong with you or why you can't live the life you were meant for. That fire inside of you of personal potential, the one that craves growth, challenge and getting out of your comfort zone – tucked safely away while you stay in the bubble of your world, swiping, scrolling, watching, slowly mentally dying.

To me, that's much worse and that's the toll that our digital world is taking on many of us and it will only get worse with the advent of the unregulated and open-source use of AI to exaggerate all of the challenges listed so far. More on that later.

What is your digital grind?

Is it always being on at work or is it the uphill battle to keep your kids creative and present? Is the phone featured as a third entity in your romantic relationship or friendships or has your hustle turned into a ball and chain rather than a road to freedom? Do you spend your leisure time staring down instead of connecting IRL? Are you slipping into a life you hardly recognize – one that is so safe and yet so afraid all at the same time?

This might be the point where you challenge me and tell me that you are totally fulfilled, perhaps have built a business from your laptop and meet people with similar interests all over the world and if so, that's great. We are all at different phases of our lives and what we need at one stage is not what we'll need at others. You may have parts of your life totally handled with boundaries and productivity hacks but like many of us, there may be another part of your life where these principles may apply.

Start where you're at. Asking yourself what your digital grind is is deeply personal and the truth is probably somewhere under a blanket of secrecy and shame. That's ok. It starts with reflecting to ourselves, admitting our own struggles with technology but perhaps on a wider scale, noticing other questions about how we live our lives.

Are we honest with ourselves about what we want? Are we honest with others about who we are or are we wearing masks that keep us isolated? In theory, technology should enable us the freedom to self-actualize. To get curious, creative and have more time not less, and yet it seems to have made most of us panic at the world and obsess at our differences rather than connect on our similarities.

I've listed only a handful of challenges above from my perspective and the research I've done but I don't actually think technology is the enemy. I'm not a fear-monger harking back to the 'good old days'... no, I do not have rose-tinted glasses about the past. I am, however, someone who likes looking into the future and learning from our experiences. I've been in the mental health space for over a decade and am here to help us find solutions for the distress that is plaguing so many of us and perhaps, without having all the answers, help us give language to the problem so that we can feel empowered to use the tools on offer that can help.

To evolve into the future, we must set out fully awake, intentional in how we want to build our workplaces and homes so that we can maximize the potential of technology while boosting our mental health. This means more responsibility placed on the business of attention fuelled by the advertisers and big tech giants, to make it easier and more acceptable to manage our attention ourselves. It means responsibility for researchers and educators to take seriously the impact on our children's diminished cognition and empathy so that we can educate and evolve with technology, developing the neural pathways that will enable us to stand tall alongside the speed of AI and other developments and effectively utilize tech to evolve our workplaces, communities and societies for a fulfilling future.

CHAPTER TWO

The psychology of digital wellbeing

So let's get to the root of things.

What do we need in order to develop into emotionally healthy, resilient and functional people? People who can use technology to their advantage rather than disintegrating into burnout or thinking that if we just find one more hack then life will be blissfully easier, and we can all rest awhile.

Potential and why it matters

I keep talking about potential. As you read this book you may be thinking, I don't care about my potential, I just want a few moments of peace.

It may look as if the world is becoming obsessed with self-help – you only have to open YouTube, TikTok or whatever platform you favour to see the rise of the influencer telling you three steps to be a better person, hack your health, meditate, sleep, take cold showers, set goals, make every minute count. You may feel exhausted by what you see as pressure not potential, so you tell yourself, I don't care about all that, I just want to watch funny cat videos, and your algorithms are more than happy to oblige.

According to the *Merriam-Webster Dictionary*, potential is simply 'existing in possibility' or 'capable of development'. The *Oxford Dictionary* defines potential as 'latent qualities or abilities that may be developed and lead to future success and usefulness'.

I like that. Usefulness can connect us to community, it can help us feel fulfilled, it can help us feel part of something and boost our mental health. Arnold Schwarzenegger titled his whole book *Be Useful* (2023), with quotes peppering the pages such as 'You have 24 hours. Use them'. If we stripped out all distraction and digital noise, how much time would we actually have in a day to build our capability and do the things that really bring us joy, the potential outlined in the definition for good mental health?

Reaching potential is about self-awareness. Canadian psychologist Jordan Peterson wrote on X (formerly Twitter) in 2023, 'You're not everything you could be and you know it'.

Reaching your potential is not about yourself comparing to others but about comparing yourself to who you were yesterday, taking responsibility for your own mental health and learning how to develop your skills and knowledge so that you can remain relevant in a fast-changing society. This has an added bonus of preventing the slow decline into resentment, frustration, depression, pain and poor health that befalls so many people, not because of chemical imbalances but because of a deep sadness and shame at not having taken that risk, said what they meant and lived a life of bravery and personal pride.

Potential can be cultivated through learning. And this is where technology can greatly enhance your experience. You have access to mentors, guides, books and teachers completely free from anywhere in the globe. This to me is the greatest benefit of technology today – access at our fingertips to free learning.

What stops us reaching potential: being stuck in survival mode

Let's start by talking about survival. This is the mode that many of us today seem to be firmly stuck in and which can make us freeze and unable to do the things that will boost our wellbeing and help us reach our potential. When I go into high-powered workplaces and talk about mental health, performance and leadership I'll generally always remind people about the physiology of survival; how your body thinks it's helping (when actually it might be glitching) – an old record of how to behave adapted onto a new world with new threats for which we have no blueprint.

We all have a primary response to danger or perceived danger, an alarm system in our bodies. Our earliest childhood experiences, parental role models and whether we felt safe as children will all play a part in wiring our brain to react in certain ways when we think we might be unsafe or are experiencing stress.

You'll be familiar with your fight or flight response – your wallet is grabbed by a stranger in the street and in a split second you react: you decide if you can chase (fight) or you run to save yourself (flight). This of course is a real danger scenario and what this reaction was made for, but these reactions show up in everyday ways too. Your partner calls you out on something, you immediately dive into debate or argument to defend yourself (fight) or you shut down, sulk, physically leave the situation (flight). You're at work, your project outcome is called into question, you immediately defend your corner, unafraid of conflict (fight), or you acquiesce and take it, deciding in your head that it's simply not worth discussing as they are more senior so must be right (flight).

There are a few other pieces too. Freeze is a more extreme survival state often made concrete by prolonged exposure to toxic stress – in the animal kingdom this would be called playing dead; in the adult world perhaps it's shutting down, feeling numb or being unable to formulate the sentences you're good at in a stress-free environment. Fawn is a recent addition that many people are less aware of – it's our survival impulse to people-please or adapt who we are to fit someone else's expectations in order to, again, feel psychologically or physically safe in the situation (Walker, 2003).

Reflect for a minute on what your go-to survival response might be. Is it fight, flight, freeze or fawn or a combination of these depending on what's going on around you and what reaction is activated?

What does all this have to do with technology?

Understanding your nervous system and survival response is essential to help you identify your relationship to your devices. It will help you assess what you need to do to reboot your life.

Translate your survival response to receiving notifications, alerts and reminders buzzing through your device which is in arms' reach at all times. A similar survival response will be activated.

We may not be in real danger, but with each alert our body needs to assess for a perceived threat, and in an age of fake news, clickbait and negativity, we may be activating our survival impulse hundreds or thousands of times a day. No wonder we're feeling frazzled and burnt out! Even if we're disciplined and turn notifications off, we may still feel the pull of survival by obsessively checking things that don't need checking just in case something catastrophic has happened that we may be missing out on.

Belonging and negativity bias

As humans we are hardwired to want to be part of something, to fit in, to belong.

Many of us are sleepwalking through our digital lives, unaware of the early influences that are impacting our behaviour and responses to the world around us; we just think this is our personality or how everyone is. When in survival mode it's hard to be strategic, reflective, creative or intentional about our habits and lives.

Instead we are stuck in a reactive loop – exasperated with why we can't be more disciplined in our work and lives, unaware that the system is set up to trigger survival impulses keeping us hooked on quick dopamine hits while fighting fires, as resting and reflecting doesn't seem like an option in our always-on culture.

This brings us to negativity bias and the compulsion to watch the horrors of life rather than soak in the good. According to the Center for Humane Technology (2021), bad news travels six times faster than good news. Anger is the emotion that travels the farthest on social media and many people are unable to know the difference between fake news and real news, choosing rather to garner information from celebrities on TikTok than understand what sources their information is coming from.

Negativity bias has its roots in evolutionary psychology, which notes that we are more likely to focus on negativity or potential threats as this would have been advantageous to survival. If you get too comfortable or complacent, well you just might be a little snack for a sabre-toothed tiger. So it's better to chill but never be too chill that you don't notice what's coming. Of course, back then all you had to do was scan the horizon or take turns being on lookout and stay within safe running distance of your cave.

Today if you don't actively and intentionally focus on the good and switch off the negatives, the world will decide for you and surround you with panic, mistrust and fear.

Remember that creativity and innovation mostly show up in environments of safety. So reaching potential, as the wellbeing definition highlights, is about moving from a place of woe and into a placc of trust. However, as the world polarizes us more and more, it can often feel safer to the survival body to stay in a tribe (any tribe!) even if it means giving up our values, our voice, our soul.

Braving the messy middle and taking ownership of our lives

How do we counter the pull to just follow along with the crowd? As Dr Brene Brown states in her book *Braving the Wilderness* (2017), true belonging is a spiritual practice; it's about the ability to find sacredness in being a part of something but also the courage to stand alone.

This can be scary of course. Putting down our devices and listening to our body can feel like listening to a stranger if we've lost the practice of just being – without distraction. Yes you may have more health data than ever before telling you how you've slept, what your heart rate is and what your nutrition needs or stress levels are but even these hacks can mean the neural pathways that connect to the internal knowing of your gut have atrophied. I can't remember phone numbers anymore because that task has been taken over by my device. In the same way we may just lose touch with our inner knowing when the data is doing the job of telling us how we are.

Often, we avoid sitting with ourselves because we're afraid of what we might hear. Our inner voice might tell us to leave the relationship, the boss, the toxic environment, the addictive habits, the unhealthy friendships or behaviours that are holding us back from our potential. We're afraid of the messy middle and so latch onto a three-step influencer hack on how to feel better rather than experimenting with what is right for us. In *Women Who Run with Wolves* (2008) the price we pay for inaction is highlighted. Clarissa Estés states, 'It is worse to stay where one does not belong at all than to wander about lost for a while and look for the psychic and soulful kinship that one requires.'

We're so scared of that middle bit. The wandering a little, lost for a while, while we unlearn and relearn to attune to who we are deep within, the voice that comes in the stillness when all hacks and tools have stopped. I'm not saying to give up technology. I'm saying to look up for a minute to figure out who you are and your responsibility in creating the life you want and then intentionally use technology to help you get there.

Being seen: developing early attachments

Without going fully into all developmental psychology, I think it's worth noting a few foundational points.

Firstly, we all want to know that we are 'normal' humans and there's nothing inherently wrong with us. As many of my therapy clients say as soon as they first meet me, 'I had a good childhood and my parents did their best'. I'm like, nice to meet you too and then quickly reassure them that when we look into our past it's not about blaming some kind of evil perpetrator who purposely messed up your life, it's simply about acknowledging your story and influences so you can better know who you are and decide who you want to be.

No parents or environments are perfect and it's a relief to know that the great child psychologists agree with British paediatrician and psychoanalyst Donald Winnicott's findings on 'good enough parenting' (Dethiville, 2018) – that's it's even good for parents to not be perfect as this allows the child to deal with challenge which in turn builds resilience and allows them space to cope effectively in the real world later on.

There have been some fascinating studies, however, on the elements that support good enough parenting and enable us to develop into healthy adults, and which I was able to study at length in my Master's in Psychodynamics of Human Development at Birkbeck in London. A major factor is our attachment style, which is formed with our primary caregiver and then shows up in other relationships over and over if not noticed and consciously adapted.

In short, it is essential that we are seen by our primary caregiver, that the funny baby voices are made and that the child sees that you see them – it's like they aren't a whole person yet and that act of being seen makes them begin to feel whole. We need touch, we need eye contact, we need safety in order to develop in a healthy way.

What are attachment styles?

To simplify, there are four main attachment styles. You can read a decent summary of them in relation to our adult love lives in the book *Find Love* (2024) by global relationship science expert for Tinder, Paul Brunson.

Secure attachment

Let's start with the healthy one, which, yes, does exist and which roughly 50 to 60 per cent of the global population do exhibit: secure attachment.

You'll know you tend to this attachment style if you're at ease in relationships, are good at communicating feelings and are able to be vulnerable and open with others.

Avoidant and anxious attachment styles

We then have anxious attachment and two types of avoidants – fearful avoidant and dismissive avoidant.

Anxious attachments would be identified through relationships making you feel anxious, unsafe or insecure as you likely have an unconscious fear of abandonment or being left.

People with a fearful-avoidant style may find relationships chaotic as they veer between being anxious and avoidant. Finally, dismissive-avoidants find intense emotions overwhelming and they can often pull away from others (flight) – deep down you desperately want to connect to others but stressors in the relationship lead to arguments and lead you to pull away and withdraw as this feels safer.

Remember all of these styles would have been a very young child's way of coping with whatever environment they were thrown into. If you were not able to have eye-gazing, play and connection (even through life circumstances such as a mother's postnatal depression, parental work, volatility in the home, a grieving carer, etc), you will teach yourself very early on not to rely on these things for survival, instead learning to self-soothe and essentially sort yourself out – which can show up in adult relationships as keeping things to yourself, avoiding interpersonal conflicts under the guise of 'being independent' and not trusting help when it is offered.

Why attachment is important in digital wellbeing

What does this developmental process have to do with your relationship to technology? In Lindy Cundy's book titled *Attachment and the Defence Against Intimacy* (2018) she notes that if you are of the anxious or avoidant natures, 'Technology can provide a means of connecting with others, but also functions as a screen between self and other, or a filter so relationships and intimacy can be controlled. It is possible that digital technologies are creating a more avoidant society.'

Just think, if every time you feel a little bit anxious or uncomfortable in a life situation (such as standing in a line at the post office) or within a friendship or relationship and there is a risk of rejection, risk of intimacy or being vulnerable and you have this handy option to avoid that uncomfortable feeling that is both addictive and entertaining – well, for many of us we're going to take it. While you might think, well yes, what a relief to look busy and not have to have the awkward conversation or make eye contact with someone, we have to also wonder what this is doing to the skills we need to thrive in the world today.

Cundy continues that what's great for any kind of fear or anxiety, specifically for those of us prone to anxious or avoidant attachment styles, is that 'technology is more or less reliable and predictable, which makes us feel good. In public spaces, being engaged with a screen creates the illusion of existing in a bubble, preventing the approach or intrusion of other people. Technology provides a kind of psychic retreat.'

While on some level technology enables us to connect with more people and the skilled among us can ask the difficult questions and nurture intimacy, for many of us, the opposite is taking place. Working remotely, swiping for connection and utilizing emojis as a form of communication, without realizing it, we can descend into a loneliness we can't quite describe – something akin to a lack of belonging or simply being seen for who we are, not the avatar version that we present to the digital world.

It's not all doom and gloom

Thankfully we can actually evolve our attachment styles as adults with some awareness and practice, and there are real benefits in technology when it comes to being honest about what we're going through. I spoke with digital health expert and activist Kat Cormack Jackson, who reminded me that technology can actually save lives:

> When I was young and struggling with my mental health, technology literally saved my life and that of others… but of course those were the days of anonymous forums, where your experience could be more anonymous, but living in an isolated space struggling with my mental health, I could find people to talk to who could understand.

While young people's lives are more likely to be presented publicly these days, it still stands that in many homes or communities the first place someone might be honest about experiences of poor mental health or their experience of being marginalized may very well be online, potentially with other likeminded people who can hear their story, maybe for the first time.

There are also sites (such as those sharing self-harm methods or suicide ideologies) which can be extremely negative. However, we must also hold on to those places where it's easier to be ourselves or seek help online – at least at first.

Think of the young person who is contemplating their sexuality in a highly conservative, remote or religious town, feeling alone and hopeless – access to the wider world through technology offers hope and can offer a community where there is no hope of one where they are. They can be seen in a digital space where it is unsafe to be seen in person.

Assess where you're at and what you personally need

In managing a digital landscape, here's a few questions to ask yourself:

- What are the important parts of my story that impact my behaviour such as my attachment style?
- Do I turn to technology for self-soothing when I'm bored, tired or nervous about connection?
- Am I losing the skills of being with myself and reaching out for connection because it's easier not to?

Asking ourselves direct questions, discussing them in our communities and being radically honest is the first step to assessing whether our digital world is beneficial or is robbing us of the opportunity to build resilience and necessary skills for engaging effectively in the adult world. Awareness is always the first step to experimenting with new ways of being.

Burnout, crash points and danger zones

This may sound odd, but I believe crash points and rock-bottom moments can be wonderful things. It's where the cracks show, the habits are forced to be reckoned with and an opportunity arises to truly remind yourself of who you are, what you want and what is possible. Of course, it doesn't feel like it in the moment – it mostly feels confusing and awful and like nothing makes sense.

For many people, it's only when they can no longer cover up the pain that they decide to wake up, change something in their lives or ask for help. And so, there's something beautiful and hopeful about these challenging times.

Symptoms of depression, burnout and anxiety or whatever life challenge you are facing (change, divorce, physical illness, etc) are life's opportunities for growth.

Digital burnout

Burnout is classified by the WHO (World Health Organization, 2019) as a workplace phenomenon with symptoms such as energy depletion and exhaustion, mental distance from your job or feelings of cynicism and reduced professional efficacy or effectiveness.

Digital burnout or technostress is commonly defined as a modern disease of adaptation caused by an inability to cope with new computer technologies, affecting mental health. It is also defined more generally as any negative impact on attitudes, thoughts, behaviours or body physiology that is caused either directly or indirectly by technology (Bondanini et al, 2020). Those negative impacts can be viewed through the burnout lens of energy depletion, exhaustion, cynicism or reduced effectiveness. I'm pretty sure we can all relate to this experience at times – you're in a meeting, your phone is pinging, you have email notifications on your desktop, slack messages jumping on the screen and perhaps a WhatsApp group begging for your attention while your wearable is telling you it's time TO BREATHE!

Hitting a crash point can have dire consequences on your lifestyle, hitting both your physical and mental health, and yet it's a pretty human thing to wait until your body orders you to stop. We know something's wrong; we must suspect it – maybe we're drinking more, sleeping less, exhausted or we've allowed all the things that used to bring us joy to slowly slip away from our lives. We tell ourselves if we can just get to this next project, job or event everything will be fine, forgetting that there will always be a next thing, a next achievement or thing to do – and what we're missing out on is, well, life.

What if our body is telling us in those moments of change or pain that our lifestyles are not matching what we need in order to recharge our focus and reboot our life. What if our mental health crisis is fuelled by our digital environments, lack of connection, poor nutrition, over-medication, addictive impulses and always-on culture and so when the usual challenges of life show up, we are unable to roll with them like waves but instead we feel hit by a tsunami and over time this leads to a crash? What if, however, there is a gift in the crash – a point of forced reflection so that we can both individually and collectively see that there may be another way?

So how do you know you're experiencing the unique blend of technostress and burnout that generates digital burnout? Here are a few ways to assess yourself and what might be playing a part in your experience, ideally long before you reach a crash point:

- **Information overload**
  When we're in a place of constant exposure to a large volume of information, notifications and updates, our brain can feel overwhelmed, not knowing what to focus on in order to survive so it feels scattered and hypervigilant.
- **Continuous connectivity**
  The internal or external pressure to always be reachable both professionally and personally can reduce time to be present, focus on your body or create the space to reflect on what you need.
- **Multitasking**
  Research suggests it takes 23 minutes to fully refocus after a distraction (Skillicorn, 2023) so in the modern world are we really dealing with less time, as so many of us complain, or are we simply managing more distractions, so it feels like time is slipping through our fingers?
- **Social media pressure**
  This comes back to that tribe vibe. We want to be part of something, we're afraid of missing something important or not being seen and counted in the digital world – so we post, like, comment, watch, compare rather than really being present and living in the moments that make up a good life.

- **Digital distractions and sleep**
  Have you ever spent an hour scrolling only to realize it's way past your intended bedtime and now your sleep is disrupted, and when you finally do fall into a restless sleep, you wake up tired and irritable? You kick yourself for once again going down the vortex of distraction and perhaps claiming next time it will be different, you'll stick to your bedtime routine, switch off effectively and so the cycle continues.

You may be able to list some more challenges such as learning new tech, restructures at work, being separated from your support networks because you live on a different continent or a feeling that you need to always be tapped into the news. It's the stacking of things over time that leads to those burnout symptoms. So ask yourself honestly, are you on a fast track to burnout (exhaustion, cynicism and reduced effectiveness) and does your relationship to technology play a part?

Ask yourself, which of the above challenges might be showing up in your life and where do you need better knowledge, support or boundaries? What is in your control and what is out of your control?

Don't worry too much about your crash point; instead, learn to listen to the information within it.

Are we responsible for changing our relationship to technology or is it a bigger issue?

In this chapter I've highlighted our own responsibility when it comes to digital wellbeing; we must be honest with ourselves, recognize our danger signs and assess our own relationships to devices.

But in a world where the system is set up to compete for our attention, is it really just *our* responsibility to change from within or does the wider system have to answer for some of our symptoms of poor mental health too?

There's a great meme that's been doing the rounds which you may have seen. The picture is of a koala hanging onto a chopped-down tree shaking in absolute terror, surrounded by a forest of chopped-down trees. A man is pointing at the koala while his assistant takes down notes. The man says, 'This koala has a mental health problem' and of course the message is clear. It's not the koala's fault, it's the fact that his environment has been decimated and he is having a reaction to this decimation.

In a family or work culture, the same can be true. When things go well, parents or systems take credit for their excellent guidance but when people show up with negative symptoms, we say things like, I just don't know what happened, there's something wrong with them, they should just use the resources available, it's all on them.

In the same way, we as individuals should be responsible for our relationship to our devices, and practice healthy boundaries. However, we must also look at the collective squeeze that is pushing so many people into this position. Has the system simply cut down all the trees and then tried to fix things with productivity apps, perks and helpline numbers?

This isn't about blaming the system fully or not taking responsibility for ourselves, it's about recognizing the business models at play that are competing for our attention and highlighting the impact on our psychology, making it harder to enforce the boundaries that look so easy on paper.

If you are hating on yourself for being so weak as to let these devices impact you it's honestly not all on you. As long as the business model for apps (yes even wellbeing ones) is to compete for your attention or sell you things, well there's only so far our willpower can take us – we will end up like the alcoholic who has tried all the ways to manage their drinking and yet, eventually, still ends up blacked out in a heap wondering what the hell happened this time.

In order to create mentally healthy cultures, we need both individual and collective responsibility. There is hot debate, led by the Center for Humane Technology, that is asking for greater legislation and support for the challenges we didn't know we needed support on before. It's easy to keep our head in the sand about the impacts of technology and potential threats of an unregulated and open-source world of AI and yet, as I've been immersing myself in this topic, there are many elements we must wake up to if we are to evolve in a way that benefits society in the future.

Summary

Knowing your attachment style and asking yourself reflective questions about your story that may be impacting your willpower or ability to be intentional about your digital usage is essential to using tech for good instead of it using you.

Digital burnout is real and is really the cumulative effect of many years of stress and trauma stacked on top of each other that finally affects your physical health, usually in a stark way that can take years to recover from.

Crash points, whatever they look like to you, can be blessings in disguise. I'm not saying all bad things are blessings; what I am saying is that when we hit our own crash points, whatever that may be, there is an opportunity in breaking open and letting the light in.

Ideally, we want to see these crash points coming in order to wake up and develop an early warning system that gives us insight into when to adjust or change our lives so that we stay in alignment with our true selves. Granted, there's a lot of noise these days so it's harder than ever; there's pressure to conform, to stay connected, to live lives of quiet desperation and so the trick is to turn down the volume just a little in order to be reminded of who you are and what you need in order to thrive.

CHAPTER THREE

Comfortably numb: Overcoming digital malaise

Writing this book coincided with six months of heartbreak. My kids moved away, my partner and I broke up and after a whole life looking after others, here I was, in my one-bedroom flat in South London sitting with, well, myself.

I am usually a pretty boundaried and focused person, but during this emotional time dealing with normal life challenges, I found myself spending more and more time scrolling pointlessly through YouTube shorts, Instagram or even checking emails when I knew there was nothing important and it was the weekend. The act of holding onto my device and having somcthing to do felt urgent, an easy way to not sit with my painful feelings.

Many readers will have been there. There might be an elephant in the room that needs to be addressed, or we might be experiencing grief or heartache and may be aware that there are messy feelings lurking within us but instead of feeling them to the fullness of their capacity, we go inward and do the easiest thing in front of us: shop, scroll, swipe and check. We may even know clearly and unequivocally that this is not making us feel better and yet there it is, a comfort.

Symptoms of digital malaise

You'll know you're experiencing digital malaise when you start experiencing symptoms that can be linked to excessive interactions with digital devices or online environments.

You might notice that your sleep is disturbed, your thinking more anxious or you're missing out on the things you know support your wellbeing such as meeting with friends or moving your body. Instead, we stay in, watch one more Netflix show and reactively grab unhealthy food, avoiding the people who might challenge our behaviour. I'm not advocating for pretending everything is ok or showing up at life running and skipping if that's not how you're feeling, rather, if we have a device that can so easily help us avoid feeling difficult feelings – well then, many of us are going to enthusiastically take this option. What we don't realize is that instead of solving the issue through processing (which, yes, means actually feeling everything and reframing our thinking around it as well as learning from the experience), we end up stacking all these unprocessed emotions so that they can affect us in a much more major way down the line.

I recognize I am a case study of one. I can usually after a day or two put things in place to pull myself out, refocus where I want to spend my time and ask myself what I really need. However, during this time in early 2024, I stayed up long after I'd usually go to sleep, nervous of the loneliness that waited for me, tired but not wanting to be left with the thoughts that would remind me of change. I just kept watching snippets of distracting information, telling myself that at least my algorithms are set to feed me self-help and workout inspiration. I told myself that this was a step up from negative news, funny cats or celebrity gossip – and yet, the time was still sucked away and I still stumbled to bed digitally fried.

'Is drink costing you more than money?' is a popular Alcoholics Anonymous (AA) catchphrase. I know you probably don't see yourself as addicted but out of interest, switch the word drink to *digital* addiction. Let's assess our own connection to digital malaise by reflecting on these sentences, copied verbatim from the addiction guidance and meant to help you assess whether you may have a problem:

- Has digital addiction affected your relationships with your family, friends or former or present employer?
- Has digital addiction affected your health?
- Has digital addiction affected your state of mind?
- Have you become preoccupied with your digital devices?

If you answered yes to one or more of those questions, then digital malaise is impacting you and it's important to reflect on other tools to help you refocus and reboot your life.

How our devices are keeping us stuck

Our digital devices have become our comfort blanket, our escape, our connection, even our friends. The trouble is, when our devices help us avoid really feeling and processing, thereby moving us through painful times quicker, we lengthen the process and stack the un-felt feelings for later. We might avoid reaching out and nurturing meaningful connections or engaging in the activities that will support our wellbeing, instead favouring what is comfortable instead of useful.

If you know your story, your triggers and what life experiences affect you most, you may have seen a shift over the years in how you move through your challenges. Are you able to sit in the simple discomfort of waiting in a queue for example? Are you able to feel your feelings or has it just become so much easier to avoid those icky human vulnerabilities – things like grief, boredom, anger, sadness, fear, melancholy, envy, loneliness, etc. We know that technology has changed our lives and mostly that's no bad thing; however, the crucial thing to note is how your responses to normal life problems have changed too.

Just go to a concert or a school play to notice how much our responses have changed – rather than sit in the moment capturing the memory in our senses, we capture everything on our phones, watching even our real life in the moment through a screen. There are other things that may seem silly too. We're more likely to Google search for information or find out how the world works on our social platforms rather than talk to someone and share ideas. While on the face of it this is an efficient way to learn, it also seems to be robbing us of valuable skills that help us negotiate time and space with other people in the world – maybe it's robbing us of the skills to be human.

To challenge digital malaise, we must embrace our humanity

To be human is to feel, to think and to connect. It is to know the richness of emotion – that is, what it is to be alive as a human. Digital malaise impacts our human spark and our ability to connect, it robs us of the energy and creativity to engage in the world in a way that boosts our overall experience of being alive – the pain and the joy. Instead we get flooded with overwhelm, chasing the next dopamine hit of a like or purchase, but it never quite feels as good as the first time and while you'd be correct in saying that it's not such a big deal, it's just entertainment, it's when life hits challenges that many of us use our digital lives as a crutch to avoid ourselves.

How our earliest experiences shape us

As Alain de Botton says in his book *On Love* (2006), 'Perhaps it is true that we do not really exist until there is someone there to see us existing, we cannot properly speak until there is someone who can understand what we are saying so in essence, we are not wholly alive until we are loved.' Our earliest experiences shape who we are and how we engage with the world.

As the infant who needs to be seen by their primary carer to understand themselves – so too do we put out bids for connection all the time so that we can make sense of our world. However, so often our bids for connection through our varied digital communication methods fall short of the mark. Emojis, emails, voicenotes and all the varying messaging channels might offer part truths but can lead to misunderstandings, ghosting and, of course, loneliness.

In order to challenge digital malaise we must become a bit uncomfortable. Let's face it, being able to order food to our homes, work from home, connect, shop and basically do everything from the comfort of our homes gives us great freedom but also keeps us cocooned in a cave where resilience to life's struggles is unlikely to build. In order to boost wellbeing we must question if our digital landscapes are enhancing our human needs or if this ease has become a route to hide and thereby atrophy the skills needed to keep us well.

These skills start with self-awareness and developing a sense of self-identity. For those of us who did not gain a healthy sense of self from our early experiences, we may have a tendency to disassociate from ourselves – to avoid our inner world of feeling, as deep down we don't think it is safe.

'Dissociation is a distinctive sign of a weak sense of self entailing a variety of amnesiac mental tactics for evading mental realities,' states Oliver James in his book *How to Develop Emotional Health* (2014). 'Dissociated people,' he continues, 'escape from the present by becoming distantly absorbed in a single aspect of the inner or outer world', going on to describe that traumas that occur before the age of two can predict whether an adult is more inclined to dissociate in their adult lives.

Knowing our story is key to understanding how the digital landscape can more easily be used to help or hinder our lives. Abusive or neglectful childhoods can impact the ways we develop our sense of self and make it harder to negotiate what is real and what is fake online. This means that young children may be piecing together a sense of self from their screens rather than from their parents' gaze and in turn find it more difficult to understand their emotional world, instead actively avoiding this difficult task. These children then turn into adults, joining a changing workforce without the skills to engage on a human level.

The digital world is set up to enable us to dissociate as much as possible so that if and when a life event happens that is difficult, if we are too focused in a digital space, we have not built up the skills to understand our emotions, communicate them effectively, sit with others within the pain and move through the darkness in a way that allows us to build resilience, emotional capability and enriches relationships rather than sinking us further into isolation.

Making life easier or better?

We need a level of discomfort in order to grow, change and evolve as humans. When you go to the gym you essentially make your muscles very uncomfortable for a short time in the hopes of making yourself more comfortable later, by boosting your physical health, confidence and attractiveness. In Maslow's hierarchy of needs he outlines the basic needs that must come first (such as safety, food, shelter, etc) in order to then give rise to our growth needs such as cognitive function, self-actualization and transcendence.

For all the negativity in the world today, statistically we are safer and healthier than we ever have been in many areas of life. Our day-to-day lives in western societies and even many places globally are simply more comfortable than ever before. We can order meals or groceries straight to our door, work from our homes, shop through our apps, live in warm spaces and date by swiping and texting rather than walking up to someone and asking them out.

We are sold quick fixes for our health, hacks for our wellbeing and we actually have an inordinate amount of time to stay on our devices without the threat of being eaten by a predator or losing our livelihoods. While there are many horrors that take place in the world, on the whole many of us do not fear for our safety on a daily basis and have space through digital efficiencies to sit around in contemplation.

For most of us, however, what does all this contemplation time do in the modern world? Well, it mostly freaks us out. When we contemplate the big questions of life for many of us, we feel pretty overwhelmed as this entails also contemplating things like death, suffering, meaning and potential or perhaps we have to acknowledge our own part in the demise of relationships or the life experiences we are having.

All this can feel pretty intense if your sense of self is a bit wobbly and so rather than do the hard work of feeling, radical honesty and sitting with the paradox of what it is to be human, we have a world we can slip into, dissociate from our feelings and avoid these rather messy human thoughts. Instead of enjoying our relative comforts, we play Candy Crush on our commute so that anything, yes anything, can distract us from the messy middle; we can believe through what we consume that the nuances of life can be fit into three-step frameworks and hacks keeping us comfortably numb.

When we're in survival mode, as discussed in previous chapters, we want to grab on to as much certainty as possible. The gurus and influencers we follow, as well as the algorithms feeding us, all reinforce our belief systems. We see more and more people talking with great certainty as if one perspective is total facts; the more the perceived chaos around us, the more we find comfort in knowing a truth and can surround ourselves with a tribe that echoes our point of view. It's easier to belong, even if it's in shared hatred of an opposing side.

As CS Lewis (1942) says in *The Screwtape Letters*, 'Hatred has its pleasures. It is therefore often the compensation by which a frightened man reimburses himself for the miseries of Fear. The more he fears, the more he will hate.' So in the age of the keyboard warrior coupled with a lack of self-awareness and time spent dissociating from our own emotions rather than developing a true sense of self, we are working hard to stay as numb and distant from life as possible – even when hiding behind an opinion fuelled by hate.

But that doesn't make it better.

I remember when I had a baby and a toddler and my now ex-husband and I would take them out on the weekend. We would stop at a petrol station and they would be restless and need a break and my ex would say, 'I'll just jump in the shop on my own' and when he saw my face questioning the logic of keeping me trapped in a metal cage with our restless offspring he would say, 'It's just easier'. Of course, I would think or rather scream in my own head as I hadn't quite learned to have a voice yet – EASIER FOR WHO?!

Sometimes the short-term ease with which we make decisions isn't the best for our long-term happiness. We are now divorced.

Getting the foundations right

Emotional health, healthy relationships and a feeling of wellbeing include a few key factors that we must be intentional about in order to build our sense of self, our agency and a life that we want to live. The Five Ways to Wellbeing researched by the New Economics Foundation (Aked et al, 2008) has some universal findings about what helps to build this initial foundation of wellness, including:

- **Be active.** Moving our body is the single best way to manage stress, reduce burnout and support physical vitality and yet we've all wrestled with the internal struggle of not wanting to move – but if we push through the ease of sitting on the sofa, we gain a wonderfully natural dopamine high that rewards us for our efforts.
- **Give back.** People sometimes say it's selfish to give back because of the immense satisfaction it can give to the person giving. Personally, I think why can't it be a

win-win? When we give to others in small ways or large it boosts our own sense of purpose, potential and belonging while also helping the other person feel seen, heard and valued – what have we got to lose?
- **Keep learning.** In our digital world, we have access to the greatest teachers in the world right in our living rooms. What an opportunity for learning and growth! Utilizing this opportunity is a wonderful way to create positive accountability and a sense of belonging with other like-minded seekers.
- **Take notice.** There's a lot written about mindfulness, meditation and training our brain to let go of thoughts and be right here. Whatever your practice to train your brain, the real test comes in real life. Can you bear to leave your phone turned off while out with a friend? Can you stomach watching a concert without recording it? Can you be in a work meeting with no distractions? This is the ninja level of taking notice in the world today and is the most evidence-based way to train your brain to focus.
- **Connect.** Connection can't only happen during performance reviews at work or on holidays with loved ones. Connection is a daily practice of bravery that allows us to notice what is going on around us and connect emotionally with other humans. This doesn't have to just be bad emotions as sometimes assumed in our mental health-obsessed culture, it's also about sharing joy, gratitude and how we can support each other through the wonder and pain that is life. Connection is a brave act and one that we can start today.

It takes radical honesty to see our part in things and where our desire for comfort is trumping our desire for wellbeing. Comfort and ease are ironically not the same as wellbeing and thriving. Not always anyway.

We often think of wellbeing as bubble baths, self-care, maybe a spa or lighting a candle. And while yes, I have nothing against these things and they may very well be part of how you invest in yourself and boost wellbeing, if we're going to effectively navigate our mental health crisis in a faster-paced digital world, we're going to need a bit more embracing of discomfort to help us thrive.

So what are you saying, Petra – choose discomfort? A friend of mine when going through a difficult time was joking about the different mindset and movement tools that were advocated to help her get through a phase of melancholy and joked that it was all good and well but there was no way she was doing any of these things *every day* – what a ridiculous thing to suggest! And so she stayed firmly attached to her sadness when there were clearly a few simple things that, if done frequently, could support moving her to a happier place.

We were laughing about it, but I also suggested, with kindness and care, that perhaps this was a belief system that was keeping her stuck. As we talked it struck me how much our brain is not on our side! Our evolutionary brain's purpose is simply to keep us safe and in a digital world of ease this often means telling us to stay in our cave, order in and keep our doors locked.

In its quest to keep us safe our brain will do everything in its power to convince us that another hour in bed is great or grabbing that sugar-fuelled snack is a great idea; it will tell us we absolutely NEED that item on sale and we should definitely stay in a social media war to channel our hate in the misguided belief that convincing total strangers that we are right is time spent in purpose – after all, we're doing the world a service and them a favour.

What we need to understand is that we must challenge the thinking that easier is better and instead choose discomfort. If you want a chance at protecting your brain from distraction and boosting your health and creativity, you're going to need to figure out how to delay gratification and focus on the things that matter – not the billions of things actively competing for your attention.

The commoditization of emotion

Let's talk about how our emotions are used to keep us in digital malaise. The commodification of emotions for commercial purposes involves the ways in which businesses and marketers capitalize on human emotions to drive consumer behaviour and increase profits.

In his book *Sedated: How modern capitalism created our mental health crisis*, James Davies highlights how our distress is being commoditized, with our innermost emotional states online being used as data to feed us distraction and get us to buy things:

> When we suffer, we are not encouraged to delve down and face reality; we don't learn about what is broken in our lives and society. We are not taught to read, to think, to struggle, to act. Instead, we do what our economy wants – we reach for the consumer products that falsely promise a better

life for a price – the entertainment, the clothes, the pills, the stuff. We don't manage our distress through action but through consumption.

How is this done you ask? Countless ways really, but here are a few to think about:

- **Emotionally charged advertising**
  Marketers often create advertisements that evoke strong emotions such as happiness, nostalgia, fear or excitement. Emotional appeals can be more persuasive than purely rational ones, making us as consumers more likely to remember the brand and feel a connection to the product. Just think of Coca Cola and the feelings you get after you watch their ads. They generally feature joyful moments, celebrations and togetherness, creating an emotional association with the brand.
- **Emotion data mining**
  Companies collect vast amounts of data on consumer behaviour, including emotional responses, through social media interactions, online activity and biometric data. This data is used to tailor marketing messages to individual preferences and emotional states, increasing the likelihood of engagement and purchase.
- **Engagement through emotional content**
  Social media platforms thrive on user engagement, which is often driven by emotional content. Influencers and brands create emotionally engaging content to attract followers and drive sales. The algorithmic nature of social media platforms amplifies content that evokes strong emotional reactions, leading to more visibility and influence. For example, Nike's advertisements frequently use inspirational messages that evoke emotions

of empowerment and motivation. By aligning the brand with athleticism, perseverance and success, Nike creates a strong emotional bond with its consumers.
- **Emotional branding**
Brands create identities and narratives that resonate emotionally with consumers. This can involve aligning the brand with certain values, lifestyles or causes that consumers feel passionately about. Emotional branding helps foster brand loyalty and encourages consumers to see the brand as part of their identity. For example, Apple's marketing strategies are a classic example of emotional branding. By creating a strong brand identity and fostering a sense of community among its users, Apple has built an emotional connection that drives consumer loyalty and repeat purchases.
- **Experiential marketing**
Companies create immersive and emotionally engaging experiences around their products or services. Examples include themed retail environments, interactive online experiences and branded events. These experiences are designed to create positive emotional associations with the brand.
- **Creating emotional dependency**
Companies design products and services, particularly digital ones, to create a sense of dependency. Social media platforms, video streaming services and mobile apps often use notifications, updates and personalized content to keep users emotionally engaged and coming back.
- **Manipulating emotional responses**
Neuromarketing uses insights from neuroscience to craft marketing strategies that directly influence

consumers' emotional responses. Techniques such as eye tracking, facial coding and EEG are used to measure emotional reactions to advertisements and products, allowing marketers to refine their approaches for maximum emotional impact.

Just look at that list and see what we're up against. No wonder it feels impossible to just put boundaries in place or hack your relationship to your screens as if you're somehow weak and deficient when you fall into the rabbit hole. There are literally billions of dollars spent on making sure your boundaries don't work. No wonder the struggle to get our wellbeing foundations consistently right also feels like a much bigger issue than ever before.

Renowned clinical psychologist Dr Anne Cooke notes in conversation with James Davies, 'The mental illness narrative encourages us to see mental health problems as nothing to do with life and circumstances, so no wonder we don't look at structural and social causes.' She goes on to say that the notion of pointing the finger at individuals to reform themselves to fit in with social structures as opposed to understanding the structures that are oppressing us is one of the biggest things we're getting wrong about mental health today and I have to say I agree. While I am completely for taking responsibility for what's in our control and not having a victim mindset about the circumstances around us, I am also for waking up to the world around us and the systems at play.

If we don't know what we're up against it's really hard to create a plan to tackle the challenges and learn to thrive using the great bits of technology that could help. We must work with and continue to refine our structural boundaries by working with places like the Center for Humane Technology to begin to structure ethics around the use of emotional commodification and collectively protect our attention.

Knowing what we're up against, it's totally understandable that we are overwhelmed and deciding to remain comfortably numb.

With the speed of technological advancement, it can be hard to know how we even begin to tackle this rate of change. Like many of us, I've definitely been guilty of keeping my head in the sand and keeping my world as small as possible in order to live my version of a good life, and I don't think there's anything wrong with this per se. The downside comes when there's a terrible trade-off, one of being isolated and lonely, which more and more of us are feeling in a hyperconnected world. We keep the struggle firmly internal, thinking everyone else must be thriving while we struggle to manage our lives, blaming ourselves for our poor mental health rather than collectively looking at solving the context around us.

How to challenge digital malaise

So how can we notice, reflect and act when it comes to our propensity to remain comfortably numb? It sounds like we need to make life harder, not easier. That if we sit back and let life happen, we will inevitably get sucked into the vortex of commercialism, expectation and eventually mentally check out. Creating change starts with honesty – simple but not easy when we're in the practice of avoidance. We must ask ourselves, are we sedating ourselves by managing our symptoms or are we taking a proactive approach to nurturing a life that is awake to the full emotional range we are gifted with as humans?

Remember that even the seemingly negative emotions are loaded with information to help us lead lives beyond 'quiet desperation' and lean into our growth potential. As Dr Brene Brown says, 'I think the most terrifying emotion for people to feel is actually joy'. It's like the human condition experiences full unbridled love and joy and then immediately squashes that feeling in fear, thinking, what if I lose it, what if something bad happens?

Her research highlights, however, that the more we experience joy the more resilience we actually cultivate that will help get us through the tough times when they do inevitably occur. So, if the tough times will definitely happen and we can't avoid them, don't you want to also fully experience the good bits of what it means to fully be alive? Love, adventure, connection, playfulness, music, art and community? For some of us these days, to engage in the real world feels loaded with risk but that's simply because we're out of practice. Just think, if we numb ourselves to the bad feelings which eventually could evolve into worse things like depression or anxiety, we also end up numbing ourselves to beautiful emotions, the ones that make life worth living.

So the task is one of experiencing and acknowledging our emotions. The task is one of bravery and showing up to life.

The task here is to be brave enough to sit with your feelings and let them pass through you. This doesn't mean you have to act on every feeling or thought, it's the journey of understanding your emotions and separating out past emotional triggers from current emotion information, integrating these personal ideas into who you want to be today and how you personally want to show up in our digital world.

What's recently helped me is journaling. No journal prompts, no framework to follow or a 'right' way to do journaling, just a simple blurt onto the page allowing me to process the messy scrawl of wonderings. Tearfully holding the middle truth on these pages, that love was powerful and real in my relationship, it taught me so many things and even though the distance is right for the next phase of life, it's ok to grieve, to feel and to let go.

I know full well that if I don't feel these feelings and process these emotions, they will stack within me as walls when the next opportunity for joy and love comes along – that resentment will build into a story of blame or pain rather than one of grief or gratitude. So I choose to experience the beautiful and sometimes painful process of being alive, remaining open to trust and love again.

Try asking yourself how comfortable your life is and what you could do to create just a little more friction. While this may seem foolish on the surface, creating a little discomfort or sacrificing a little on the front end leads to great possibility on the life end.

Summary

We need to wake up. If we can understand the challenge, we can more easily work together to create solutions as opposed to suffering in isolation, unsure how so much time is lost as we cycle in a system set to commoditize our emotions. We must reclaim our humanity by owning our own feelings, challenging influence and choosing discomfort rather than staying in the nice warm comfort blanket that eventually atrophies the muscles of connection, health and hope.

Notice your exhaustion, really feel it and understand its influences. Once you understand yourself, your triggers, strengths and weak areas, you can make sure you dial up your wellbeing foundations and nurture the right kind of connections around you.

Let's dive deeper into how the machine holds us back and what to do about it in the next chapter.

CHAPTER FOUR

Set up to fail?
How the machine holds us back

Growing up in a cult there were a few patterns that I see replicated in many workplaces and family systems today. When an individual goes through burnout, depression, grief, anxiety or whatever human challenge, we immediately point fingers (either to their face or mostly behind their back) thinking they really should have known better, be doing better, change their lifestyle, mindset, habits – essentially, we blame them for how they are feeling and why it is taking so long to feel better.

If someone is obese, for example, we might judge them as lazy and simply not listening to the very clear advice from their health provider. We often don't take into account the context within which they live. Experiencing a traumatic event could affect an individual's willpower as they struggle to understand the impact on their body, causing them to self-harm through overeating. Rather than judgement or being told they're not strong enough, they may actually need a trauma intervention and an understanding of the context in which they live: living in a fast-food nation, with processed foods being advertised to solve their emotional needs.

The context matters and I call it the machine. The machine that is holding us back – a context that is much greater than simply thinking about willpower or hacks to improve productivity and focus.

Using a business example, let's take someone in the workplace. They have been taking days off for illness which is actually an undisclosed mental health issue, and the manager is exasperated, saying, we have a helpline, self-help apps, meditation offers or training – why are they so burnt out? They're just too lazy to use the tools on offer. They must not be a culture fit or are simply lazy, weak willed and can't cut it in this industry. We don't take into account their workload, a toxic manager, endless meetings, lack of fulfilment in their jobs, lack of trust in senior leadership and being pushed to their absolute limit. The context is burning them out and yet we blame them for their lack of focus and attention and poor use of random crisis resources that the workplace offers.

We also don't take into account that many helplines treat people like numbers, support often has enormous waiting lists or very short-term interventions and utilizing an app to boost wellness can feel isolating and takes an incredible amount of resolve, especially when struggling with any number of real-life problems – which sometimes all come at once.

We all live in a context, an environment that plays a part in how we feel.

What cults can teach us about the machine

You may think a cult is a pretty extreme comparison to the machine that is holding us back; however, my experience of both holds some distinct parallels. If someone in the cult I grew up in was physically ill, perhaps had doubts about the way we did things or was mentally distressed, it was very clearly a *them* problem and would elicit prayers, isolation, cruel punishments or even excommunication. It was *their* fault – no responsibility was taken by the environment, relentless belief systems, ever-changing rules and intense working practices that could drive someone to be experiencing said distress. The system was never at fault. However, paradoxically, when something went well (a big win, a new donor, a new disciple or other such proofs of concept) all credit was taken by the collective, their way of life was validated and leadership were seen as doing the right thing, leading well and inspiring appropriate action.

In the space of digital wellbeing I am seeing the same dynamic.

If you are burnt out, addicted, overwhelmed, depressed, comparing is impacting your self-worth, you're broke, gambling or feeling more anxious or less able to focus, society will instruct you on your responsibility to have better willpower, to create better boundaries and criticize you for simply being a weaker human who hasn't handled modern progress in the way it was intended.

But the system is set up against us and wants to see us give away our focus – by which I mean, mainlining information and distraction and capturing our attention so that we can be sold to.

It's like saying to someone with an alcohol addiction that their boundaries are at fault once again: just have one drink and avoid the spiral of doom that is soon to follow; you've got this; Instagram said there's just a three-step formula to follow and you'll be a balanced drinker. With my own alcohol addiction issues, I know that my conscious choice is at play but I'm also genetically predisposed to go overboard after the first drink, so managing my alcohol intake just never worked. Instead, my boundaries had to be more extreme – never drink again. I realize I'm coming at this from the furthermost end of the continuum but I'm not the only one – the context of addiction exists and impacts more of us than you may think.

Is digital detox the solution?

Due to the extremes of digital overwhelm, we must turn our minds to resets, rehabs or digital detoxes. Are these the solution? While of course some of us can self-impose a digital detox, this can feel like it's for the privileged few. We have businesses to run, children to keep track of and life to be on top of.

According to Johann Hari, the best-selling author of *Stolen Focus: Why you can't pay attention* (2023):

> Digital detox is **not** the solution (to our tech addictions) for the same reason that wearing a gas mask for two days a week outside isn't the answer to pollution. It might… keep at an individual level, certain effects at bay – but it's not sustainable and it doesn't address the systemic issues.

A digital detox may not solve systemic issues but if you've ever tried one before it can act as a glorious reset. A reminder that there is a whole world out there if we just look up long enough to really take it in.

If we're going to influence real change, however, we must influence the system. This can feel totally out of reach, though – how in the world do we impact a billion-dollar machine, how do we just keep our focus and stay sane alongside consumer marketing and attention competition? Thankfully there are some things we can do as individuals to manage our focus and attention and I'll go into tips and ideas for managing your relationship to technology in future chapters. However, it's important that we are alert to the system at play and practise a little self-compassion as we all experiment, for the first time in history, with evolving our boundaries, our knowledge and cultures to enable us to ensure technology helps us thrive for better rather than for worse.

'Come on,' said a friend to me recently when learning I was embarking on this topic, 'if we can't even manage the pull of notifications, how in the world are we going to manage the pace of change brought by AI?' Totally fair, I thought. The world of technology isn't slowing down.

I wondered, though, if rather than attack the machine or blame the individual, making it an us-vs-them problem, it might be useful for us to embrace an explorer's mindset. Rather than taking sides in the argument and placing full blame in either camp, we could instead embrace open discussion, the sharing of honest experiences and acknowledging that none of us has been here before. This is a brave new world and while there are always haters when something new shows up, those who thrive are those who are adaptable, willing to hold the paradox of healthy and unhealthy and collaborate on making the digital world safer for our children's developing brains as well as evolving us into a new world of work fuelled by connection and structures to help us focus.

Cults and the need to belong

When doing my research, I interviewed a former Google employee and posed a question, saying something like, 'Do you feel whole teams of people are sitting around boardrooms trying to figure out how to make devices more addictive?' I was picturing a sort of Austin Powers figure circa 1997 asking explicitly about how the minds of their consumers might be controlled.

She replied that while she definitely saw the addictive qualities, that was not how she experienced it while she was at Google. This makes sense to me. I don't even think sitting around the boardroom discussing explicit manipulation tactics occurred in the cult I grew up in – instead it's the slow boiling of the frog analogy. It's the idea that if you put a live frog in a boiling pot they will think 'oh no' and jump straight out, but if you let them swim around in a cool pool and then put the heat up slowly, the poor frog simply won't be able to tell that the temperature is rising and instead becomes *cuisses de grenouille* (a French frog-leg dish).

The environment I grew up in felt normal to me because I'd been there long before the water started to boil. I couldn't tell how weird things got because they were always a little weird; coercive control was just adults being in charge, playing my part in the commune was just my duty as a citizen, believing the world was going to end was just that, the truth. And when the second coming never happened when predicted there was always a seemingly rational reason for why that was – God is pleased with you, he has shown mercy on the wicked and is giving them more time to be saved, your job is doubly important now and so the cycle of the next second coming would ensue and hey, we just kept swimming.

I needed all the symptoms to show up before I could jump out of the pool. I didn't know the source was being in a toxic cult but instead I felt anxious, depressed and was leading a double life playing the good girl on the one hand and hedonistically escaping on the other. I wanted to tackle these *symptoms* because symptoms are annoying and I thought that if I just tried harder then it would all make sense – but of course it didn't work that way.

The thing was, it wasn't always horrific. There were good bits too – a shared mission, connection, music and clear roles that gave an illusion of safety. But there was also propaganda feeding our belief systems on a daily basis, which influenced my view that this was indeed normal and everyone 'out there' was actually at fault.

This seems extreme as an example to most people, but I think the principles in this extreme apply to the broader cult systems we are in today. You just need to remember Steve Jobs' iconic introduction to the iPhone in 2007 to remember his cult following, making the Apple brand about belonging and feeling part of something, not just about technology. It's only in recent generations that tech progress has moved at such a pace that we are playing catch-up and are trying to adapt quickly to the new normal. We've been creating a whole new pool with a whole new temperature and are still figuring out how to acclimatize to it in a way that doesn't 'boil the frog'.

Wellbeing hacks: selling solutions to man-made problems

I am all for progress and the endless benefits we could list about how tech has been used for good in all corners of the world and yet we're all figuring out what the new normal is and, importantly, how our wellbeing and brain chemistry are impacted. One of the worrying things is how mass information is informing our belief systems, and most of it is influenced by consumer marketing – those smart people sitting around scheming for ways to influence the consumer (you, me and our children) and convince us we need products to make us happy.

Product placement is the norm and for the first time in history kids are marketing to other kids. They are not old enough to have the life experience necessary to discern what products they are offering others but are fuelling the machine, believing that more is better and if you only had this product to keep up with the Joneses (which is no longer just on your street but every street, everywhere) then you would be enough – but of course, there's always the next rung of the ladder. As soon as you get to this level you now know you have three more to go and on and on our world of dissatisfaction goes.

We deem this normal, swimming in a pool of acquiring more things, more stuff, more experiences, more self-help, more wellbeing hacks and more tools to help us manage the world we're in. We use more drastic tools to manage the symptoms that are stacking in this mental health crisis, hardly questioning the environments that brought us here.

Yes, I did in fact add acquiring more wellbeing hacks to that list because in a world of information overload we're even being sold that more wellbeing tools will give us the satisfaction we crave. We feel we're doing wellbeing wrong if we haven't ticked off our list of hacks such as cold ice plunges, workouts, meditation, gratitude practice, journals, connection, intention, manifestation, productivity hacks, etc. You get the idea!

I am definitely for all of these things in their own time and if they suit you and the phase of life you're in, but there's an additional point. It seems like a lot of these hacks are solving problems created by the systems around us and perpetuating this need to use our devices to consume hacks to support our focus and wellbeing. All of these tools can have benefits, but sometimes we need to question the environments we're in that are making us feel like somehow we're doing wellbeing wrong even when inundated with millions of simple hacks. It perpetuates the idea that our symptoms are our fault while assuming that everyone else is somehow getting it right, making us hide in the shame and blame of getting it wrong.

When writing this book I had the privilege of staying with friends on the island of Madeira in Portugal. Their house overlooks the ocean and is surrounded by banana groves and impressive cliffs framing the view. The air is different up there and the simple act of zooming out on the immensity of nature and hearing the gentle lap of the waves in the distance had an immediate mindfulness affect – I am here, I feel grateful, everything makes sense, I can breathe. No app necessary. I immediately found it easy to leave my phone in my room or stay present even though I was on a working trip and putting in my word count at the same time. I hadn't changed as a person, but my environment had. Perhaps my influences had too as the household I was in took a flexible approach to work and projects, choosing their schedule based on the weather that day as to how they would focus their time. We were incredibly productive but in a way that listened to our own needs, our body and aligned with the world around us.

When I left cult life at the age of 22 I cut myself off from everyone in my past for a number of years. I did this because I had no idea how to think for myself, how to make healthy judgement calls on the environments I found myself in or how to know what my needs were much less put in boundaries to ensure I could thrive. We can't just thrust an app into the hands of someone who has no idea what a healthy boundary is or how to manage the epic responsibility of their digital wellbeing and the risks attached to consumer marketing, without educating them on what exactly to guard themselves against.

I've had people tell me there are no dangers in our relationship to devices because the phone companies have created many tools for managing notifications, alerts, productivity time, etc. And sure, there may now be tools to help us manage things but first, why are these tools being created? Because on the whole we are seeing evidence of damage being done when these things are not managed so tools are popping up to show that responsibility is being taken even though, according to the Ledger of Harms (Center for Humane Technology, 2021), many tech leaders won't allow their own children time on devices due to their inside knowledge of the addictive and debilitating effects on children's brains.

Stress and misinformation

And then there's stress and how it impacts our ability to think in any kind of rational way and do the things that seem so simple on paper. (It's not technology's fault, just have a better work-life balance and set boundaries for yourself! Be disciplined!)

In Dan Ariely's book *Misbelief: What makes rational people believe irrational things* (2023) he highlights how 'Stressful conditions tax our cognitive bandwidth, reducing our ability to think clearly and exercise executive control. Stress also hurts our ability to make rational long-term decisions that require delayed gratification.'

Stress is not the enemy of course – good stress can help us fuel our potential and thereby enhance wellbeing. However, these days I'm seeing people so stuck in survival mode as outlined earlier that we are in states of extreme stress, impeding our ability to think in ways that could help boost our wellbeing. When I do talks and ask people how they invest in themselves they're likely to list all the classic ways to improve focus and productivity (sleep, exercise, nutrition, doing something they love, etc); however when we're in unhealthy stress, we're more likely to turn to the unhealthy coping mechanisms rather than the good ones – insert your preferred poison here.

We'll reach for the sugar, yell at someone who doesn't deserve it, experience road rage, gamble, drink, watch countless hours of TV and on and on that list could go, including slipping right into what consumer marketing had in mind all the time – becoming susceptible to emotionally manipulative advertising with stress impeding our ability to make rational decisions, thereby buying more.

Groupthink

Why can't we just do something about the systems around us so we can collectively manage our wellbeing and focus, you might ask? Something that plays a part in our systems and structures is how we collude to keep things the same. We all do it; even in healthier environments we're likely to experience groupthink.

Groupthink is about thinking or making decisions as a group, resulting typically in unchallenged, poor-quality decision making – it's a phenomenon that occurs when a group of individuals reach a consensus without critical reasoning or evaluation of the consequences or alternatives. It's based on a common desire not to upset the balance of the group.

Why does this matter to the topic of digital wellbeing? Well, I think we're colluding on making everything individualistic, hyping up the benefits of tech and not effectively challenging each other in our workplaces, relationships and homes when we feel that connection or productivity is lost.

Take meeting culture in a post-covid world, for example. My team and I work with hundreds of organizations globally and if we talk to people individually, they will echo the inefficiencies of meeting culture by saying things like:

- Meetings are just put in my diary out of core hours due to time zones or senior leadership availability, not considering my workload.
- I'm in meetings all day, which means I end up doing my actual work outside of hours.
- I sit in so many meetings that feel pointless. My energy just crashes and I feel no motivation for my work as I'm not even included in the meeting.

You get the point. Collectively everyone just seems to accept that this is the way it is and nobody wants to rock the boat or be seen as difficult or risk their jobs. It seems to me that many workplaces are colluding with practices that are grossly inefficient and leading to overwhelm, absence and burnout and yet nobody is doing anything to change this approach – just layering on resources or outsourcing wellbeing hacks, which doesn't get to the root issue.

In cult life, abuses of power go unnoticed, marginalized groups continue to be stepped on and anyone who questions the belief system is ousted or made an example of. By the same token, corporates have policies, processes and simply 'the way it's always been done' practices that equally mean abuses of power go unquestioned, marginalized groups are stepped on and anyone who questions the belief system is put on a performance review, given grind work, ignored or even restructured out.

Groupthink and how we relate to others

When's the last time you asked someone who was checking their phone during a dinner or a hangout – not to mention in your primary relationships – to be more present with you and less distracted? Sure, we may snap from time to time, 'You NEVER listen' but we often don't communicate to the root issue – I don't feel seen by you when you're emailing and busy with your phone, I feel invisible and like there's no point in me being here. You know what we often do – if they're on their phone, we pick up ours too.

And so, our circles of influence become just like our algorithms – repeating back to us what's just easier for us to do or watch.

The reason I bring up groupthink is to further wake us up to our own part in the system of behaviours that keep us stuck and to begin to provide some solutions. We struggle with loneliness, digital overwhelm and unhealthy types of stress at work and yet so few of us are truly questioning the way we're doing things, instead frozen in information overload and emotional marketing, feeling too small to create any real difference. Instead we just accept things the way they are.

We are in uncharted territory, AI escalating us into unknown places that will radically change the skills needed to thrive, so it's imperative that each of us takes ownership over our resilience, our thinking and evolving our wellbeing practices to sit alongside this rapid change while also collectively questioning the systems around us.

Artificial intelligence

'Can AI act as a useful therapy replacement and show the kind of empathy needed to give people who are struggling access to support?' was a question I was recently asked after a keynote. I've been asked for advice on this topic for white papers, therapy apps and self-help tech tools over the years and it has generally given me pause as I think about the technical aspects of mimicking empathy and the power of actual relationships to support good mental health.

You may have an immediate reaction yourself, either for or against pseudo empathy mental health tools. The reality, however, is nuanced and while it seems logical to have an opinion, there's just so much we don't know that it's hard to fully comment.

What we do know is that AI is here to stay and is moving faster than our legislation can keep up with. There are stresses linked to how it will impact jobs, the skills that we'll need to develop and some very real worries that are being spearheaded by Tristan Harris and Aza Raskin from the Center for Humane Technology that we would be wise to take heed of (Harris and Raskin, 2023).

Looking at the potential risks is like an abyss of madness that it's hard to sift through. Headlines like 'My AI is sexually harassing me' (Cole, 2023) and 'Algorithms are making decisions about healthcare which may worsen medical racism' (Grant, 2022), as well as rogue chatbots being named in the spread of misinformation (Hsu and Thompson, 2023), are all very real challenges that we must navigate collectively.

By the time this book is published anything I write on where we are with AI and its risks will already be irrelevant so rather than focus on the worries, I'll focus on my expertise, which is the wellbeing and mental health agenda linked to AI and the two questions I usually get asked:

- Are we right to be nervous of the implications of AI on our mental health?
- Can AI be used for good to support our mental health and provide access to early interventions that can be more cost-effective and scalable in our growing mental health crisis?

Just like with anything the technology itself doesn't seem to be the problem – it's of course how humans use it and to what end. I think we're right to be nervous about AI and certainly it's important that we educate ourselves, protect our children and back organizations like the Center for Humane Technology, who are trying to ensure these things are developed with safety in mind. With deep fakes, hoaxes, reports of suicide linked to chatbots (Walker, 2023) and predatory and discriminatory language, we are right to question the impact of this technology on our collective society and mental health.

Living in a state of perpetual fear and stress is also terrible for our immune system so it's not useful to be sitting in fear, especially about things that are not in our control. So it's crucial that we don't spiral into overwhelm, obsessing about the digital vortex and going down a rabbit hole of clickbait to help us make sense of things. We must strike the balance between awareness and focusing on what's in our control, prioritizing habits that can support us to stay creative and focus on what matters most in our world.

AI therapies and support

Back to the question. Can AI be used for good to support our mental health and provide access to early interventions that can be more cost-effective and scalable in our growing mental health crisis?

There are early studies that highlight benefits and the effectiveness of mental health support using AI – for example, a 2022 journal studying the effectiveness of AI-based chatbots in mental health support highlighted the shortage of mental health professionals as a key driver, with AI-powered chatbots emerging as a promising solution to bridge the gap in access to care (Molli, 2022). It concludes that these interventions can contribute to symptom reduction, enhance user wellbeing and increase access to care;

however, further research must be done on limitations. Generative AI will respond in a way that is constantly learning from inputs, which means it is less possible to predict whether it will remain empathetic and therapeutic or will eventually go rogue and give terrible advice which may be taken as professional advice to the untrained mind.

Mental health still holds terrible stigma in many places, so for people who are lonely and unlikely to reach out to a human therapist, a chatbot can be a useful way to offload and have a feeling of being heard. Just like writing our thoughts in a journal or talking them through on a voice note – better out than in!

The process of saying or writing what we're feeling helps us find clarity, feel acceptance and often find a way through. According to a 2017 report by the relationship experts Relate, one in eight adults don't have close friends – that's a staggering amount of people who simply have no one to talk to about what's really going on for them. Many others who have struggled with their mental health have told me that the first place they began sharing their story was online, on an anonymous forum or somewhere where it felt the risk was reduced in being truthful and real. As mentioned earlier, this action can often be the first step in building the momentum needed to get help from a human or growing the confidence necessary to take action on improving your own mental health.

In order to nurture the healthy backup some of these tools can provide, we need robust methods of research and legislation to protect privacy, prevent discrimination and ensure the limitations of the service are clear. We need to ensure people who are vulnerable and desperately looking to relieve loneliness or debilitating mental health problems are offered ideas that support cognitive processing and encourage them to do those standard healthy things – the things that have been healthy since the dawn of time: engage with nature, connect with humans and move your body.

Again, this is not an exhaustive look into AI and the varying research and experimental approaches to wellbeing, it is simply a nod to what is predicted to be the biggest disruption to how we work since the Industrial Revolution. Personally, I welcome the change. Our education and work systems have been broken for a long time and this may be part of what shakes things up; however, with all new technology it's crucial that we learn to think for ourselves so that we can navigate this world of information in a way that is healthy for our own bodies and minds. Learning how to engage with these tools in a healthy way while sense-checking what is supporting our individual and collective wellbeing is crucial to fortifying our minds in a world of distraction.

Summary

There are many parts of the machine that seem set up to hold us back:

- Consumerism is still king and set up to make us compare and feel like we'll never have enough, keeping us in a constant state of striving, never quite feeling like we're enough.

- Misinformation and groupthink are preventing us from collectively taking responsibility for the structures and ethics needed to support those of us who are vulnerable or unskilled in understanding what is real and what is marketing.
- We're focusing on individual symptoms rather than taking collective responsibility. When we focus on selling solutions for symptoms such as low mood, anxiety, tech addiction or burnout, we are keeping the problem in the lap of the overwhelmed individual, missing the point of a society that is perpetuating a state of dis-ease.

A key component of dis-ease in our urban societies is loneliness. A lack of meaningful connection, replaced instead with distant digital connection or bots is one of the biggest threats to our wellbeing. Let's tackle loneliness and how to boost connections in the next chapter.

CHAPTER FIVE

Fighting loneliness and finding humanity

I remember an argument with an ex-boyfriend about phone usage. From my perspective, he brought his phone to bed, put his ear pods in at night and shut me out, had his phone in the bathroom, on his commute and it was an isolating barrier in our relationship. From his perspective, I was always on my phone, ALWAYS working, texted people while we watched TV and was hardly ever present. Both of us had plenty of times when we weren't on our phone and connected with each other, but the experience was that when one of us looked at the other, if they were on their device, instead of saying, do you mind putting your phone down so we can just hang (which would feel vulnerable and risk rejection in the moment), we would glance over at the other (in a bid for connection) and rather than take the risk, would pick up our own device to self-soothe and distract.

Here and there this behaviour had no consequence but over time a rift grew as all the unsaid things piled on top of each other and resentment built up. What we're really looking for as humans, just like in those early stages of development, is to be seen – to have our world reflected in the eyes of someone else. Only then do we feel we really exist.

I observed myself acutely in my breakup in 2024. Armed with the knowledge of years of mental health study and experience I felt strong and as if my observation would enable me to distance myself from the pain of the breakup, reframe the experience and, as they say, move on. Well, while I definitely spent hours journalling to reframe, something curious happened during the withdrawal phase – my skin felt funny. A sort of dehydrated pulsating that longed for touch, like my skin was crying. I felt my ex's phantom presence and missed the small things that I'd taken for granted but really the living organism of my skin felt it too and it suddenly made sense to me that loneliness can literally shorten our lives and affect our physical health.

You may be familiar with the studies done in the nineties on the child development of institutionalized children – specifically those in Romania after the collapse of Nicolae Ceauşescu's regime in 1989. One of the most notable researchers involved in this work was Dr Charles A Nelson (2014), who conducted significant studies on the developmental impacts of early institutionalization on children and discovered the profound negative effects of a lack of human contact, including developmental delays, attachment disorders and cognitive deficits. These studies were done on extreme deprivation; however, the conclusions of these and other studies noted that when basic needs of food and shelter were met but there was no touch, no cuddles, eye gazing or care, children simply didn't have the essential nourishment to keep them alive – their skin and organs slowly gave way.

Thankfully, most of us won't fall into this camp and if we had touch and eye gazing when we were younger, we can certainly withstand a breakup or being alone for stretches of time – we are stocked up, as it were, and that carries us through. However, with loneliness statistics on the rise (GilPress, 2024) this is a real issue to consider when thinking about our digital wellbeing.

'I talk to people all the time,' you might think, 'so then why do I feel so disconnected or lonely?' You might not even be able to put two and two together and label it as loneliness; something just doesn't quite feel right. Maybe you feel physical pain, headaches or a sore back and you rationalize that it must be because you're doing something wrong, not hacking your wellbeing enough or that *you* simply aren't enough. All of these elements can give us information and if we really listen to that part of ourselves, we might just notice what these mixed-up feelings are saying: 'I'm lonely'.

You are not alone

You are not alone in feeling this way. There are varied studies stating that urban cities are lonelier, with factors such as noise, overcrowding and lack of green spaces contributing to this phenomenon. Even young people are experiencing higher loneliness than ever before, with social media cited as a key cause.

Loneliness is defined by the distress that results from discrepancies between ideal and perceived social relationships, so loneliness is an issue of expectations versus reality. A contributing factor may be that we're seeing other people's idealized versions of their social lives on screen vs the reality, which is skewing our expectations of how we should feel in a bigger way than ever before.

In a remote and hybrid world we can applaud the autonomy and efficiencies of being able to work in new ways and yet for many of us we're feeling more isolated than ever. Even going into offices two days a week doesn't solve this emptiness as for many of us, we come in only to be on virtual meetings all day, missing the opportunity for the connection we crave.

According to psychotherapist Stephen Westcott (no date), if you're worried loneliness is affecting your life, here are some signs to look out for – some may not be as obvious as you think:

- excess spending – managing feelings with shopping;
- weight gain – managing feelings with food;
- excessive bathing or hot showers – seeking the feeling of warmth that might be missing;
- your friends are lonely too – misery loves company and can be self-reinforcing;
- excessive TV/YouTube/TikTok binges – this is a distraction tactic rather than fulfilling a basic need;

- feeling tired or stressed often – of course, this can be caused by other things, but it is also linked to loneliness, that feeling of flatness that comes from the absence of something important;
- frequently feeling physically unwell – our mental health affects our immune system so if we're down emotionally, we're more likely to get ill physically.

In order to tackle our symptoms, we must get radically honest. We must get to the root cause of what we're really feeling so that we can find useful solutions that don't just tick a box, but that tackle the systemic issues impacting how we feel. Our lack of meaningful connection and personal contact – a lack of being seen, heard and valued by others.

Quantum energy and remote work

Having built a fully remote team, I am a firm believer that it is totally possible to boost feelings of connection from a distance. Being brave, asking deeper questions, showing care and that you want to listen are all possible virtually, of course they are, but these methods can't ever take the place of touch or energy proximity to another human on a cellular level.

What do I mean by energy, you may ask? Is this a fluffy hippy hangover from my past, you may enquire? Nope. What I'm talking about is science. Check out Dr Joe Dispenza, eminent leader in the field of neuroscience, epigenetics and quantum physics – the study of matter and energy at the most fundamental level.

At our core we are energetic beings. We are connected by the energy that vibrates in and all around us. Einstein even referred to a physical phenomenon known as quantum entanglement, a 'spooky" experience of energy being connected even from miles apart. In one of the most famous experiments in quantum entanglement, algae cells were grown together in a petri dish, then separated in half, one half being brought to a lab miles away. When a low-voltage current was applied to one half of the cells, despite the distance and separation, the other half responded in the exact same way, instantaneously. What is so brilliant about these experiments is that they show instant communication between not only subatomic particles, but living cells, separated by miles, and so it is possible to truly experience energetic connection even through technology.

A friend just called me from the other side of the world. He called because he's going through something deeply personal and felt I would be someone who would understand. We talked about the past, our triggers and managing difficult family members who simply don't understand our worlds.

We spoke for an hour about deep and meaningful things, no video, no direct energy proximity, but still at the end of the call we both reported physical sensations due to the depth of the conversation. Slight triggers, huge pride at how far we've both come and love, really – he was emotionally regulating his breathing and my hands had a tremor and needed some movement to rebalance my energy.

It felt like energy pulsating between us – true and meaningful connection making each of us feel less alone even though we are literally on opposite sides of the world. In proximity we may have had a hug or eye-gaze but that's no guarantee we would have touched on everything we did or felt the same energy between us.

It wasn't the technology either that guaranteed this experience; it was the risk we both took to show up as humans. It was the risk we both took to be ourselves that enabled our energy to connect in a profound way.

Growing up in countless countries, houses and spaces, my family and friends are scattered across the globe and being able to stay in touch for free is epic beyond belief! I remember times when a call was simply too expensive and so we sent letters in the post, thinking carefully about the costs attached to staying in touch – and now, from anywhere in the world we just use a WiFi connection and can hear, see and… well, only those things – hear and see our friend, teacher, loved one from anywhere in the world.

It's funny how quickly things can change, too. Living in urban south London with a partner and my two teenagers, even though I worked from home, there was a natural community of friends and connections that occurred almost organically. Move us forward to 2024, a breakup, kids moving to university and three close friends moving out of the city and, suddenly, working from home while living at home alone became more of a prison than an opportunity. As a successful adult with a hyperconnected LinkedIn following and credibility in my networks, my quantum energy field had changed, and I had to grapple with loneliness on a very real and personal level.

How loneliness shapes us

My hope is to help you start with awareness and compassion for how you're feeling and observe how others in your world might be feeling too – noticing if technology is helping or hindering your connections.

No matter what it looks like on the outside, loneliness is subjective as a feeling and when noticed for what it is can feel deeply physically and emotionally painful. Our reaction might be to pull back further, isolate and hide due to the shame and taboo of loneliness as an experience. We think there must be something wrong with us and assume that everyone else is living lives of constant support and connection. If you've gone through a life change like I did, you may need to go into your cave for a while to spend time in contemplation. There's nothing wrong with taking time to be alone – just make sure you know when this pulling back begins to calcify into a habit and it's now difficult to make the first move to connect. When you're ready, there will be things you can do to move back into a place of connection but it takes emotional risk, it takes being brave enough to talk about it and go first.

Being physically alone does not have to equate to loneliness and being with people in no way means feeling belonging. We can be in a long-term relationship, surrounded by people at work, surrounded by family on the weekends and yet feel lonely. That ache of not being seen for who we are, our masks so firmly in place that we are floating through life, unknown, unseen, our soul untouched.

Why is this? How can we be hyperconnected with a free medium in our pocket for being 'with' people in any part of the world and yet our sense of belonging is skewed and our health is suffering because of this internal isolation?

The paradox of the human experience is that many things can be true at once.

Life is globalized, no longer centred around a church or community; we move homes, we change jobs and there's no immediate place to slot in to find our fit. It's also our primal need to fit somewhere, as historically we would have perished if we didn't, and so we shape-shift, adapt and be who we think other people want us to be in order to belong. Belonging anywhere seems better than floating into nowhere.

At work we join networks or cause-focused clubs; personally we have hobbies, marry into families and adapt what we see people around us doing and experiencing. We may use the pub as our place for connection, we may learn a new skill or perhaps swipe 100 times a day for the potential of romantic connection and yet here we are with loneliness and poor mental health statistics rising.

Connection: a skill to develop

To add to this, I believe many of us are simply out of practice at social skills and nurturing true depth of connection – it's a skill and an art to move seamlessly from small talk to deeper connection, to enable trust and safety to blossom so we can get somewhere and not stay stuck discussing the weather or work.

With the context of lockdowns during the Covid-19 pandemic, we then moved from isolation to navigating a hybrid world and while we've all busied ourselves with survival and adapting to the new normal, many of us still feel relief when social plans are cancelled so that we have reason to stay in our nice warm cave – social interaction feeling like a bigger effort than before.

While, in the short term, staying in more, working at home and having more flexibility is a great thing, I do often wonder if we're doing ourselves a disservice. Remember what I said about discomfort and how we should generate discomfort in our lives in order to boost our focus? It's natural for humans to gravitate towards ease – staying in and watching Netflix just feels easier than going out and engaging in the world – but is ease actually good for our mental health?

It takes courage to talk to new people, put ourselves in new environments, be the first to talk, to say hello, to try new things. It takes resilience to take action on our need for connection, ask great questions and make ourselves vulnerable. The antidote to loneliness is connection – connection is not just being around people, it's being *with* people. It's developing the skill of meaningful connection which often means being brave enough to go first, showing a measure of curiosity to the person in front of you and they in turn will usually do the same for you.

I believe this is possible virtually too; it's just about asking more explicit questions and creating the space to really see others. We must challenge the stigmas that surround feelings of loneliness and bring this topic into the light.

Stigma and taboo

Loneliness still holds a whole lot of stigma. It's funny, in many places we're much more open about mental health but less likely to say I'm lonely, isolated or need positive energy, physical touch or deeper connection.

It's like there's something wrong with us if we are experiencing these very natural responses to the environments we find ourselves in. Rather than viewing these unprecedented times as a collective opportunity for learning and evolution, we hide behind our profiles and present a picture of social ease and high status, all the while suffering behind the screen.

We compare our insides to other people's outsides – a sentence I learned in Alcoholics Anonymous when I first decided something needed to change in my life. We do it all the time; we think they must be smarter, know better, be better. We have even coined a term for this idea… imposter syndrome. Let me tell you, of the hundreds of therapy and coaching clients I have seen over the years, many of them highly successful, they all felt someone else was doing it better or knew more. All of them. When you talk to high achievers and look beyond the glamour behind the scenes, you'll find that everyone is just making it up as they go along. It's everyone's first and only go at life. We are all learning as we go so nobody has it all figured out – there simply isn't enough time.

When I first became single, as is my way, I began reading books on embracing singledom, finding love or enjoying life as a single person. Hilariously, I noticed that when I was on the London Underground, I would hide the book titles, ensuring the cover was folded over or my bag was strategically placed on my lap to cover the title. What in the world was this about? Why, as a purveyor of authenticity, would I care if someone on a train noticed I was reading a book about loneliness or being single?

Well, shame really.

It was the idea that they would be tut-tutting in their heads or looking me up and down in judgement instead of a assuming I was the successful commuting stranger I was hoping they'd see. Obviously, none of them were paying any mind to me at all, instead focusing on their own self-obsessions, but it gave me some insight into the real taboo of this topic and made me focus on the skill of honesty when people asked me how I was.

For many people, even if someone gives them condolences on a breakup or a change in life and asks them how they really are, for the brave who are honest they might say something like, 'Yeah, it's hard, I'm adjusting... but don't worry about me, everything happens for a reason and life is good and fine, etc.'

Why do we say how we feel and then quickly cover it up under niceties? Why do we avoid words like lonely when describing what we're going through? Because we don't want an awkward interaction, we don't want the other person to feel responsible for managing our difficult emotions and we are protecting ourselves from the shame of this admission – maybe we haven't even really admitted it to ourselves as we somehow feel like a flawed human if we are lonely.

What I've learned to say, only if it's true and honest, is something as specific as possible. Here's another way I might reply to a friend: 'To be honest it's been a tricky time; some days I'm really excited about my future and feel it's the right thing and then other days I have self-doubt, feel really lonely and like my skin is in withdrawal from human touch… it really can change every day – thanks so much for checking in.'

People think if they're honest it has to be a pool of despair and tears or a cover-up to make it sound better, but to be really honest is often a paradox. Many things can be true at once and honesty can simply be communicating that paradox. We can feel lonely or experience grief at one loss while also feeling grateful for our friends, our purpose and other good things. We can feel sad or disconnected in one area of our life, while nurturing a community, volunteering or building our dream at the same time.

It's ok for your paradox to change from day to day. It's ok to reassure your friend that there's nothing they can do to change it, but you appreciate them asking the question as it's nice to have the experience acknowledged.

If we were all a little more honest we'd likely find other people experiencing what we're experiencing and be able to collectively tackle this global challenge.

How we can take responsibility for our wellbeing

Human emotion is not the enemy – in fact, it means we're really alive and not dissociated from our human experience. Feeling is a good thing and gives us information that we can decide what to do with. I think we can be honest and uplifting at the same time and support each other to build community and have our needs met even though many of us are going through challenging times.

Let me explain. I used to live firmly as a victim. I told myself that convincing everyone that I'd had a tough life and therefore would be in a poor mood and self-medicate was my version of honesty – however, what I was really doing was surrounding myself with people who would validate my feelings and enable me to stay in my victim place. No one ever challenged me to take responsibility for myself or do things that were in my control – of course they didn't, because I didn't hang out with the type of people who would.

Over time, though, my circles got smaller as fewer people wanted to hang out with that kind of repeat heaviness and the doom narrative – it was, as they say, a drag. When people slipped away, I could reinforce the notion that life was hard, I was misunderstood and the world was a terrible place, thereby feeling lonelier still.

Authenticity is the quality of being real or true and I'm all for it. We need to be honest about who we are and what we need – but we need to be honest with ourselves too.

Are we wallowing in a place that is seeking validation and comfort, permission to stay stuck in an unhealthy cycle, or are we open to learning and growing as a person, taking responsibility for our own behaviour? Sometimes being honest is about protecting the truest version of ourselves. It can be healthy to forego connections that are dragging us down or keeping us stuck, but letting go and embracing that middle road can feel scary – it can feel lonely.

Loneliness might be that middle place where change occurs. The silence where we once again listen to ourselves, our heartbeat, our souls' call and we step away from unhelpful people and get ourselves ready for the next phase of life.

We must ask ourselves the same about our digital connections, who we follow and how we engage in the digital world. Are we feeling uplifted and challenged or dragged down and enabled to repeat unhealthy habits? Digital loneliness is when our expectations simply don't match reality.

We feel like we should feel better as we have loads of followers, friends and digital networks we are part of. We may compare ourselves to others' outsides while feeling the void of our insides, hiding behind our profiles and keeping the loneliness we really feel as a taboo in the shadows. How do we work with shame? We bring the issue into the light. That means openly talking about loneliness and the full experience of being human – being honest with ourselves and with others. Naming the experience means we can acknowledge the stage of life we're in and what meaning we want to give it. Is this a space of reflection, to reconnect with our centre and listen to our intuition, or is this feeling information about something that needs to shift – something that's in our control?

How to boost humanity

I held a small focus group with a group of second-year university students where we discussed the disconnection and anxiety brought on by tech addictions and it pained me to watch a kind of hopeless resolve in the air. One girl said, 'Yes, we're all anxious and I hate my phone, but I still take it to bed with me at night. There's nothing we can do about this, it's just the way it is.'

There are countless studies on the negative impacts of devices on our young people's mental health and we've highlighted some of the systemic issues that need to change, including the overall business of consumerism that is competing for our attention and thereby negatively impacting our mental health.

The other thing that's keeping us more separate and alone is the polarization of views, both by emboldened keyboard warriors and our algorithms keeping us firmly believing that one side is right and in order to belong we must pick a side too. Add on the fact that many of our nervous systems are set firmly to survival mode and you have a recipe for misunderstanding, ghosting and avoiding the messy human conversations that are necessary in order to boost true connection and create safety for authenticity.

If we're going to reduce the prediction that loneliness will become the largest national security threat in a world of AI, we're going to need to find the courage to lean in, challenge stigma and take brave action together.

As Dr Brene Brown says, *it's hard to hate people up close*. When it comes to digital polarization making us feel like we need to pick a side, we have some choices to make. We can sit back and accept things the way they are, or we can each impact our sphere of influence for good. If we individually and collectively take responsibility for the quality of our connections, in my mind, there is a future fuelled with joyful evolution rather than fear of impending doom.

Let's get back to basics and figure out how to know whether the type of lonely you feel is unhealthy and if so, what can you do about it. Remember we can be alone in a crowd so it's not so much about proximity as it is about energy. Ask yourself:

- Do the people in your life boost your energy or drain it?
- Who are you in your friends' lives? Are you the drain or a boost?

This doesn't mean being positive all the time, it means having the skills for meaningful connection and the type of honesty that collaborates and builds rather than depresses and destroys – yes, even online.

It starts with radical honesty about your habits, behaviours and interactions. There will be differences for each of us depending on where we are on the introvert/extrovert scale and what our lifestyle is, but crucially, it involves assessing digital practices and how they make us feel. Let's assess what might be in our control and what isn't by asking ourselves some key reflective questions.

Assess your digital and wellbeing practices – do you feel lonely or connected?

Here are a few questions to get you started – you might want to pick out two or three that really resonate with you in order to start small and build from there:

- How do you spend your time and how do your interactions make you feel?

- Do you sleep enough and balance your digital energy by moving your body and prioritizing healthy lifestyle practices?
- Do you have two to five people in your life who you can fully be yourself with either inside or outside of work?
- What is the quality of your connections? Are you able to say what really matters and get curious about what matters to them?
- What is your digital life like? Do you remain at a surface level across your networks and connections, or do you go deep and show up as yourself? How does your relationship with your device make you feel, who do you follow, what platforms do you use, are they enriching your connections or depleting them?
- Crucially, assess your part in your interactions and the value of your connections. For example, are you prone to negativity or being a victim of your circumstance? Do you feel like everyone else is letting you down and you're doing everything right? Do you bring real value to the connections you encounter or are you waiting for them to bring value to you?

When it comes to mitigating against loneliness there are lots of top tips and frameworks out there that challenge you to listen to music, go outside, call a friend and reframe how you're feeling.

We are all different and may need different things at different times. Sometimes being alone is good for us – it's a perfect time to reflect, re-set and listen to the voice inside you that can get drowned out by all the noise, social expectation and advice out there telling you how to live your life. Remember you are the person who needs to sit with yourself at the end of this life and decide whether you did what was in your control to live a good life – whatever that means to you.

Over my years of experience changing my own life and working with clients, here are a few universal principles that will give you a leg up in boosting connection and reducing loneliness.

Principle one: Take brave action

Healthy relationships are collaborative, not transactional. It's healthy to talk about what we need from each other and learn from the times it didn't go as well. People often tell me they don't want to share their problems as they don't want to burden others; they might know their friend is also going through a tough time and maybe, they surmise, the friend's pain is worse than theirs.

The thing is, we can't compare pain; each of our experiences, however different, is valid. When we collaborate in our trusted friendships, we trade off how we support each other and even the act of going first in discussing the struggle can give the other one permission to be open too. People often say to me, I can't believe I'm telling you this, and all I've done is share a little something of myself first and then listened fully, which has given them permission to do the same. There's no ninja-level wizardry here – it's simple. Go first. Give permission. Create space.

Principle two: Be uplifting and create accountability

Sometimes we all just need a cry, a hug and to tell someone that life is hard. What we need from them is to echo that it is indeed hard so we can let all our feelings out. This allows us to let go of the build-up of pain, grieve loss and have a witness to our vulnerability. As the witness this is a privilege and it's not your job to fix what they're going through. It's your job to be brave enough to sit in the human emotion and not try and solve it like a puzzle – you can do puzzles another time.

Having said that, I believe it's also our responsibility to be a light in a challenging world too. If we want to evolve our connection for the future it's not always about being in a doom spiral together, it's about other kinds of bravery too. It's asking what someone is grateful for or what's one good thing going on in their life, arguably maybe not during the snot-tears phase of grief, but as part of our relationship as a whole.

I am definitely one to ask my team these sorts of questions, and even with my friends I'll ask them what's one thing they're doing to invest in themselves or what's one thing in their control today. Honest! Ask them. This might seem too direct for you but for us, it enables us to move between the shadows and the light – the shadows being sometimes saying I'm so sorry, that sounds so hard, and the light being positive accountability, focusing on what's in our control: love, positive energy, movement and joy.

But what about toxic positivity, you might say? Or what if I talk about good things and people judge me or I make them feel bad? The modern language around toxic positivity means brushing over everything with a positive spin so that there's no room for negativity at all. Let's not get so scared of that, that we forget the dance of humanity: to sit in the shadows, yes, to face our fears and feelings, but ultimately to decide which thoughts we want to believe and give airtime to. From my perspective we need a little more light in the world so I don't worry too much about what others might perceive as toxically positive. This is more about comparing and feeling bad if others are doing well – I'd say there's something to be said about running your own race and celebrating when others are living in their joy.

The question to ask yourself is, what's my ripple effect today?

Did you share, connect and open up? Did you bring an energy that helped people feel loved, empowered and hopeful? This is the baseline for the connection that staves off loneliness, applicable both in person or virtually, and means we can all take responsibility for our communities.

Principle three: Check your environment

Our environments, workplaces and living situations massively impact our wellbeing. We need to assess our surroundings and what is conducive to our overall wellbeing and what isn't. It's not about escaping the cities, moving to an island with our bare feet in the soil (though science suggests that would be great); instead, it's about being awake to the influences on our life and doing small things to mitigate the harm.

Try to check in about a few things.

- Which of your senses get heightened in your living environment?

- Are there loud noises on your street, do you have a comfortable place to rest or resource yourself, what is the energy in your household?
- How does your environment make your nervous system feel?
- What's your culture and environment like at work?
- How is your energy impacted at the end of the day – do you feel belonging and connection or do you feel depleted, angry or cynical?

We spend our lives in workplaces, homes and around types of people. The relationships that form our connections, the energy that either soothes or destroys is in our day-to-day spaces. It's not just about the big things – holidays, weddings, reunions, birthdays – it's about the little day-to-day interactions that make up the tapestry of our lives and will fuel connection or loneliness.

A lonely society and how to create change

While the systemic issues in how we're working, city living and the erosion of community may feel out of our control, we have a choice to either hold up our hands in despair or to become a little uncomfortable, question the way our world is working and collaborate on using the technology at our disposal to create more connected societies.

This takes vulnerability and putting ourselves out there even though we may stumble as we experiment and not get it right at first. It takes collaboration as we share who we're trying to be with others and create shared accountability to move into a new world of opportunity. We can either resist change or we can adapt to it. This doesn't mean hopelessly falling into the traps of consumerism and addiction; it means standing tall, keeping each other honest and being the change we wish to see in the world.

Now that you've assessed a little about where you're at in the realms of loneliness and digital malaise, let's dive into real actions that can help us thrive, individually and collectively.

CHAPTER SIX

How to thrive in the digital world

Social media is the junk food of social life.
ARTHUR BROOKS AND OPRAH WINFREY –
BUILD THE LIFE YOU WANT

In order for us to thrive in a digital world we need to have an idea of what good looks like. What's our North Star, where are we headed and how will we know when we've got there? As the quote above suggests, we don't just want to chase fluff or add in more noise, apps or tools; instead, how do we get to the organic, nutritious and vitamin-dense experience of really living and allow technology to enhance the fullness of our potential?

First, we must review our relationship to technology and where we're headed individually as well as in microcosms of community. These days so much focus is put on the self that we forget that we do not thrive in isolation, we thrive in connection. It's together that we can enable a healthier experience of life with technology rather than without by putting attention on the systems and structures set up to distract us.

The tricky thing is, we can't just wipe the slate clean and start again. We must use what we've learned in this vast technological experiment and layer on legislation, protection, learning and education so that future generations can mitigate the dangers and protect their attention. We must collaborate across generations and cultures, review the very real evidence of adverse impacts on our psyche and create structures that ensure technology enhances our human experience rather than depleting it.

What might good look like for you and those around you? Let me spark your thinking by offering some clues divided into two broad categories, one of general wellbeing and one specific to our workplaces. There will be many other ways to think about what the potential of technology can be in our lives but for now let's scope out a few insights on the future.

What does good look like? Wellbeing and mental health

- Good to me is where technology is streamlined in such a way so as to prevent digital overwhelm and enhance quality of life.
- Our algorithms would expand our thinking and encourage greater inclusivity and learning rather than reaffirming polarized views. Imagine how impactful it would be if

technology boosted global harmony rather than clickbaity disharmony.
- We would be less attached to medical models of mental health and instead would take radical responsibility for our environments and our need for connection, thereby reducing diagnosis and improving mental health.
- What if we had better strategies for nervous system regulation and awareness of the addictions that play out in our tech use? What if technology offered self-help tools but also community help, prompting us to engage with a person or community in real life?
- What if our dating experiences could be slowed down and encourage true connection? What if they supported our wellbeing and gave us prompts that helped us stay brave and resource ourselves after dates?
- What if we were taught boundaries in schools? What if we learned to listen to our body and what it needs rather than outsource our intuition to search engines?

What does good look like? Work and focus

- We are more creative, feel greater team cohesion and our human skills are celebrated rather than being called 'soft'.
- We would be educated on our brain patterns and how technology affects the dopamine centres of our brain, and would create environments that could adapt to these risks by actually requiring us to take mini-digital breaks, move our bodies, knowing we'll come back more focused. Imagine if that was actually the culture,

not something you were told you maybe should think about in your own time.
- We would teach people how to manage fake news, understand the consumer agenda and learn to decide on what they need for themselves.
- We would get to a place where human creativity is protected. Imagine going into a meeting and putting all devices into a lockbox to create the conditions for full presence, humanity and creative thinking – AI is utilized for its creativity and smarts, but humans are in a place that nurtures their human potential and brings wisdom to the table.

I'm sure you could think of many more ideas from your unique perspective that would make for a beautiful utopia where technology enhances the people experience rather than creating the problems only to market a solution. I see technology as an enabler of connection, community and self-actualization only IF we're able to notice, assess and evolve our wellbeing practices and algorithms to create a future that is fair for all.

Setting intentions

Which brings us to this idea of setting intentions and taking responsibility for your digital usage in a world that is set up to keep you attached. Some people really have been upset with me while doing this research when focusing on the unhealthy elements of tech usage on our wellbeing, saying things like, 'There's nothing wrong with the device or the systems around them… the problem is our intention and not using the tools properly… *letting* ourselves get addicted.'

As someone who's been addicted to alcohol, I would love nothing more than to have found the solution to 'letting myself get addicted' and instead 'just set an intention' around my alcohol intake. I tried every intention under the sun and it still led me to the same place – destroyed. Thankfully not everyone is on this extreme of the addiction continuum and yet we need to understand that setting an intention is just a start.

What is an intention?

An intention is more than a goal or a task – it's a commitment to yourself that is tied to a purpose.

So there's a clear 'why' behind the intention such as, 'I'm going to leave my phone in the other room when I go to bed (intention) so that I can sleep well as this is great for my wellbeing (purpose)' or, 'I'm going to block out focus time in my calendar (intention) and tell my team about it so that I can write this book' (yes, that was me and yes, there's a clear why).

Setting an intention that you have any hope of sticking to needs to start with some reflection and a clear why. What is the kind of life you want, how do you want to feel, what will help you get to wherever you want to go? Assessing the big picture can help you set an intention that means something and that is really yours. If you're starting from a place of survival mode your intention might actually start with not wanting to feel certain negative things, like burnout, poor mental health or rubbish sleep. As much as I like blue-sky thinking to be about the future, it depends on what you're going through in life right now. Sometimes it's about reducing the symptoms of what you don't want first, getting yourself to a strong baseline and then reflecting on a bigger way to do what you really want.

The real skill when it comes to knowing what intention to set and making sure you're not fooling yourself is to understand yourself and learn to listen to your body. These aren't quick digital wellbeing hacks; this work isn't just a quick little tactic. It's understanding yourself deeply so you can manage your personal responses to technology and set intentions that you're likely to stick to because they're right for you.

How to listen to your body

What do I mean when I say listen to your body?

Try this. Just close your eyes for a couple of seconds, take a breath and notice what's going on in your body. A pressure here, an ache there, maybe some emotion or feeling, shortness of breath maybe. Whatever it may be, it's all information.

In a world where our bodies have been reduced to symptoms and statistics on apps and Fitbits, our mental health is medicalized and labelled and many of us are running around in survival mode, putting out fires and just getting through the day. It's like we've forgotten how to utilize this simple skill – to turn inward and listen. Even if you're an avid meditator, you may focus on your breath, you may listen to a guided meditation taking you on the journey but, still, it's often someone else's narrative guiding you rather than you guiding you. The trick is to just sit with yourself and notice what you notice. Your body is giving you information about what you need.

If you're not used to listening it may take a little while to feel confident in your own voice, but don't worry, your body is communicating – you just need to learn to listen again.

How to set an intention

When we're setting intentions around how we live our lives, assessing how technology can enhance or limit that possibility, we can sometimes feel resistance to change. I want to live this better life but if I get stressed, I'm going to just go back to my fail-safes: consuming, swiping, checking, scrolling. At least these things give me a nanosecond of relief. But these will perpetuate the same habits that are keeping you frazzled.

If you never stop to reflect, your belief system may include sentences like:

- I just can't help it
- I don't even know I'm doing it
- It's just the way the world is now, there's no point trying to stop it

For a number of my coaching clients it just takes a little unpicking and targeted questions to find out what else might also be true. That's a key question when we get stuck in a fixed mindset – we look at the news, the state of our workplaces, mental health systems, politics and just think, there's no point. Who am I to make any kind of difference? And we're doing this with the pace and speed of technological advances.

Many of us throw our hands in the air, resigned to thinking that this is just the way it is.

You set an intention starting with asking yourself what you want. You dream into the possibility of what good might look like, you listen to your body and the messages it's sending you and you adjust your life to move slowly in that direction. This is not as easy as it sounds in a world of attention competition and so the next level is less self-help and more collective support.

Discussing intentions at work, in our families, with our friends – being open to feedback, asking about the impact of distractions on our relationships and collectively holding each other to account is imperative if we're going to make real change.

So ask yourself…

- What is my personal intention when it comes to my relationship with technology?
- What feedback can I ask for from others that will help me set a useful intention?
- How can I reflect with others in my life and create collective intention?

Remember, we are in this together. Shame keeps our compulsions hidden in the shadows and yet so many of us are retreating from meaningful relationships by hiding in our devices. This is the real wellbeing crisis, a crisis of connection. And yet each of us has a ripple effect in our world where we can be the catalyst for change.

How to ask for feedback

I've mentioned feedback anecdotally, but I think it's an important topic to go into some depth. Asking for feedback helps us check our blind spots and collectively bring light to the negatives of tech usage. You might think you're pretty balanced and feel surprised when your phone tells you your weekly usage. You think that you haven't lost that many hours to your phone and yet there's the number staring you in the face.

If we're going to truly invest in our wellbeing and focus on the things that matter, we're going to have to be willing to truly listen to the people around us.

The challenge

Ask your closest people – partners, siblings, friends, parents, co-workers – how they would describe your relationship to technology. Does your self-assessment match up to theirs? Be specific in your questions, asking things like:

- How do you view my relationship to technology?
- Do you ever think I avoid interaction, intimacy or presence by distracting myself with my device?
- Do you think I'm addicted to my phone or work or a tech-based hobby?
- Does distraction affect my work outcomes?

It takes bravery to ask specific questions and then really reflect on the answers. Is the impression you're giving to others matching how you feel and how you think you're showing up? Does it match up to who you want to be and the life you want to look back on when you're old and grey?

Do you want the impact to be a lack of presence, distracted attention and multitasking at the expense of truly feeling the emotion in being alive? Do you want your kids, friends or lovers to think, 'They're a really great person, but I could rarely get beneath the mask, the busyness, the always achieving and moving at 100 miles an hour. There was that one time where I really saw who they were and then just as suddenly, it was gone'?

Do you want your colleagues at work to think, 'You know, great person, great skill but always on edge, doing emails during virtual meetings, checking their phone when having 1-2-1s'?

This isn't about comparing yourself to others. It's about looking honestly at who you want to be and the impacts of your actions so you can make conscious decisions about your intentions and what's in your control when it comes to your wellbeing and your focus.

Grassroots solutions

If you've been one of those collectively putting their hands up in despair saying, 'This is just the way the world is now', adjusting your values to the easier route of the masses, then I say this.

The world is changing at a faster pace than ever before; technology isn't going away so all we must do is acknowledge the negative impacts openly as well as embrace the positive. We know that technology can bring great good into our lives, but as long as the business models are competing for our attention it can feel like an uphill battle.

But I also think there are things we can do:

- We should talk about the downsides more, in an honest and direct way. A way that admits the cycles we're in, challenges each other's behaviour and creates positive accountability for handling our compulsions and creating systemic change.
- Get involved with grassroots solutions that are springing up across the globe. These will help respond to the challenge of disconnection and lack of presence. You just need to go on platforms like Meetup, Eventbrite, independent supper clubs, support groups or expat communities to see the varying special interest groups connecting with strangers to try mitigating against loneliness. I recently visited The Offline Club in Amsterdam – a rapidly growing movement that has spread across Holland and is gaining traction in Europe. People pay nine euros for the privilege of locking up their phones for two hours and experiencing a pre-tech world. The first half of the event is for personal reflection – reading, writing, sitting with yourself – while the second half includes playing games or instruments, art and actually talking to people around you.

So simple and so obvious. It's like we need permission and accountability to take a breath and let go of our devices; we need to know that others are taking a break too.

It's the way of history that we swing from one extreme to another before finding our equilibrium – it's the circle of life. Why not experiment with a new way of being? If you see creative spaces for connection in real life, take the brave step of joining in to see how it feels.

If you crave more creative spaces why not set something up in your local area and see what movement for change you can help create.

So how do we thrive in a digital age?

There are a few things that I believe can help us thrive. They are simple but not easy because it's not just a one-and-done situation, it's a commitment to awareness and a proactive approach that is awake to the emotion of life. It's a commitment to truly being alive.

Practising any one of these things will enable you to develop a growth mindset – an essential skill to help us navigate these fast-changing times. Stanford University Psychologist Carol Dweck (2012) defines a growth mindset as an understanding that abilities and beliefs can be developed through dedication and work, and through learning from feedback and experiences. The other end of the spectrum is a fixed mindset, a belief that abilities and tactics are static traits – you just are the way you are and can't do anything about it.

Key characteristics to develop a growth mindset include:

- persistence in the face of setbacks
- learning from criticism
- finding inspiration in others' success
- understanding that effort is the path to mastery

It doesn't always feel like we're developing these skills in the moment. Sometimes persistence just feels like white-knuckling it, learning from criticism feels like being hit by a truck, and effort feels like failure and losing so many times that we think there's no point. And yet, we get up again. That's the only trick. To face ourselves, to stay open to feedback, to keep nurturing our mind and our habits.

We might think that other people get up with more grace and therefore are getting it right – however, here's the real-talk version of what this has looked like for me over the years. Getting up has included crying while working out, using anger as fuel to keep going, watching other people do great things and thinking I'll never get there but then waking up and doing one small thing to help myself.

Mastery only feels like mastery after 10,000 hours of practice – a concept made popular by Malcolm Gladwell in his 2008 book *Outliers: The story of success* – and even then we may compare and think we haven't yet made it. Moving forward with a growth mindset isn't about grace or perfection, it's about being uncomfortable and crafting a mindset that doesn't allow knock-backs to be final; instead, it allows the challenges of life to enable growth.

I'm going to talk about setting boundaries in detail in the next chapter so for now, try to look at the following tips through the lens of a growth mindset. If there was a 1 per cent adaptation you could make, what would it be? How can you try on these ideas for size while knowing yourself and listening to your body in order to inform your next experiments? After all, that's all change can ever be, an experiment – assessing what works for you and then doubling down on that information.

Summary tips to help you thrive

- **What does good look like for you?**
  We've discussed what good might look like in general but now it's time to get granular and ask yourself, what does good look like for me personally? Do a little blue-sky thinking specific to your life. What's your version of balance, how do you want to be at work, with friends and family, when sitting with yourself? If we don't know where we're headed it's really hard to know if we got there so get detailed on what life looks like, how you feel and your impact on the people around you.
- **Assess yourself**
  This includes listening to the data points given to your body and mind. Depression, anxiety, burnout, overwhelm, sadness or trauma symptoms – if we treat these elements more like information about how we are living our lives we will reduce the focus on squashing the symptoms and instead have a conversation with our pain that can enlighten us to the change we need to make. What is your body telling you?
- **Set your intention**
  An intention is simply gaining clarity on how you'd like to be, the relationship you want to have with technology and what will support you to build the life you really want to live. Does your device and usage of technology enhance your values? For example, freedom, autonomy or family time might be important values that have been slipping over the years. Everyone will be different and that's ok – this is personal to you and will evolve at different times of your life. This is about honesty and

progress, not perfection. Naming your intention is a powerful way to make it real; telling others creates the possibility of accountability and connection.

- **Experiment**
Reflect, experiment, iterate. Relationships are living, breathing organisms that evolve over time and the same applies to our relationship with technology. It's not a fixed entity – just as soon as you figure out the right boundary, something new might emerge, your life changes and you may need to adapt. Rather than getting frustrated, like you're getting something wrong, if you understand that this is how it goes, you can flex and flow depending on what change occurs. We continue the practice of radical honesty, intention setting and experimenting as our world evolves.

There is nothing permanent except change
HERACLITUS

The one thing we know for sure is that change will always occur.

Maybe because I've been through so much change in my life, when I see people angry or resentful that yet another change has happened to them, I actually think – why are you so surprised?

It's like when British people are surprised that it's raining: 'Can you believe this weather? I can't believe this weather!' Or when people show surprise at the dark nights of winter: 'Can you believe how dark it is, it's ONLY four o'clock!!' And I'm thinking, this literally happens every year or the UK is literally known for its rain – why do people seem surprised?

I get that this is some kind of bonding ritual too and not about the weather at all, and there will be different versions of this ritual no matter what country or culture you live in; however, I think it's the same with change in our world. We say things like can you believe this government, technology, restructure at work, organizations going under, wars, toxic behaviours and on and on the list goes.

Change is just life. There are a gazillion things outside of our control so to think that anything other than ourselves is in our control feels somewhat hilarious to me. As Ghandi once said, 'If you want to change the world start with yourself'.

We must find acceptance that change is inevitable and that most things are simply out of our control. That doesn't mean we passively sit and do nothing. But it does mean we conserve our energy for the action in our sphere of influence that can create impact. So often we talk about the big changes and forget that change first starts from within.

The AA prayer says it perfectly: 'Grant me the serenity to accept the things I cannot change, the courage to change the things I can and the wisdom to know the difference.' This is a powerful statement and relies on wisdom, discernment and courageous action – and applies to all of us.

The first courageous action is taking radical responsibility for ourselves in the world: who we want to be, how we want to interact, connect and show up. If we all started there, we'd have a greater chance of recharging our focus and rebooting our lives. Leading by example is so much more powerful than telling other people what to do and yet, in a world of self-help, self-love and self-fulfilment we must ensure we then move on from the self into the collective.

We must take responsibility for building new community.

Building community

Instead of just saying what we want less of (e.g. addiction, negative uses of technology, burnout, etc) it's important to also say what we want more of.

As Johann Hari outlines in his 2018 book *Lost Connections*, 'You aren't a machine with broken parts. You are an animal whose needs are not being met.'

When we struggle with depression or other varieties of poor mental health so often our needs are simply not being met, so how do we go about taking responsibility and building the type of community that can satisfy both ours and others' needs?

Living in London, one of the biggest cities in the world, for the last 20 years, alongside the growing isolation that hybrid work and technology has brought to our lives, building community can feel like a struggle! No longer is there a simple experience of natural connection through church, neighbourhood or even work; instead, we are left to consciously decide to build community and find the depth of connection that has physical and mental health benefits.

And even with conscious decision, people move, they leave the city, they change jobs and with the best will in the world we may often feel like we're back to square one, staring at our small apartment walls wondering where our meaningful connections are.

Building community is just like anything, it's a muscle we need to keep using to keep reaping the benefits. When we take attention off something and just let it coast, we often find it doesn't just stay static; instead, slowly it atrophies, and we suddenly look up from our work or screens and wonder why we don't feel a sense of community.

What does this have to do with our digital worlds and overall wellbeing? Everything really. Understanding the practical steps for building community both online and in real life is essential – and, as ever, it's about being brave enough to try new things and disrupt our habit conversations with new ways of interacting.

Johann Hari continues, 'If you have lots of people around you – perhaps even a husband or wife, or a family, or a busy workplace – but you don't share anything that matters with them, then you'll still be lonely. What if depression is, in fact, a form of grief – for our own lives not being as they should?'

With this in mind, community and meaningful connection is not just about being with people. It's also not about having hundreds of followers, being part of networking groups or pizza and beer Fridays at a cool workplace. This all might look like community but really, it's just people buzzing around each other. Real community entails meaningful connections, which means sharing something meaningful with each other. So less how-are-you-I'm-fine and more, this is how I'm feeling, this is what matters to me, this is part of my soul.

Sure, community can also be the silences, the sharing of a task, the appreciation of another person – helping someone feel seen, heard and valued or, as my dear friend Dr Ardeshir Mehran says, 'Being seen, heard and held'. I asked him if he meant held literally or metaphorically and he said literally: 'When I have a coaching client, I will literally with permission put my hand on their back to model having their back – this creates a huge impact on their wellbeing and awareness.'

So ask yourself – where do you feel held? Emotionally or physically? Where do you feel truly seen for who you are, not a mask you wear to fit in? Where do you feel heard and valued? What is the environment that helps you feel safe enough to show who you are? These are all data points about your soul and what works for you. Listen.

It's not enough to wait for the environment to show up. To complain about lack of safety and to decry the world we live in or blame technology, bosses and others for the state of the world. This does not boost our wellbeing – in fact, it makes us part of the problem. Negativity, blame and low vibration affecting what will show up in our world.

What if we all started with creating that space for others? In my experience, when we are brave enough to open up and help others feel seen, heard and held, we get the same in return.

Not all communities are created equal

The upside of growing up in a cult and subsequently working on myself and my own biases is that I have acute discernment about healthy vs unhealthy communities. Over the years I've found the balance between noticing red flags while remaining open to experiences.

The nuance is choosing to observe, learn from past experiences but not fully armour up or decide that all communities are now dangerous places. It's trusting my discernment to slowly decide what's healthy and what isn't and make decisions based on what I need, not what a group is doing.

I definitely still have blind spots and triggers but we all do. It takes bravery to keep showing up even if we've had disappointments or some things don't go well – it doesn't mean everything will be that way. Resilience is continuing to try, move forward and open up the discussion together.

On the whole this is what I've learned about navigating new groups:

1 **Try things on for size**
Just because you like some things a leader or influencer says doesn't mean you have to accept everything they do or say. People tend to idolize someone who's said something that's helped them gain insight or have an epiphany and decide everything they say must be truth. This is dangerous and gives away our power of critical thinking and discerning what fits for us in our lives now. Test out how you feel about things personally.

2 **Be aware of groupthink**
This may feel virtually impossible at times, but awareness is always the first step. We naturally adapt how we think in groups in order to fit in and essentially survive. The trick is to reflect on your own at some point to connect within and decide how you feel about things, what fits in your life now and make decisions from a place of honesty.

3 **Follow your intuition**
I know this doesn't seem scientific and even sounds woo-woo as I bring in energy or gut instinct but in my experience, every single time I've ignored this feeling I've paid a price. These days I've even built this

concept into my business and every decision I make I ask – how does this feel? What's your gut telling you? No need for an explanation or valid argument, it just is. Trusting your gut is about learning to listen to your body. It takes time to get this right, especially if you're out of practice or have never been taught that you have wisdom within you.

Can you trust your feelings?

> *The wind that extinguishes a candle also energizes a fire*   JONATHAN HAIDT

There's a lot of hype in the self-help world about how we feel and listening to our feelings. To me there is a gut brain that is valuable and gives us different information than our cognitive function. However, our feelings can lie to us. They can be an old blueprint that hangs around long after it's useful or an indication that we are not doing the things that are in our control to help ourselves – like exercise, sleep and connection.

Feelings are useful for sure, but you need to use them as a small piece of the overall information puzzle. We need to be able to translate our feelings, to name them and understand them before deciding how we want to act.

In Jonathan Haidt and Greg Lukianoff's book *The Coddling of the American Mind* (2019), they rightly highlight that 'always trusting your feelings' is a dangerous lie and that the flame of one small feeling can be fanned into a whole forest fire of diagnosis acting as a reason to never get out of bed again – all starting with a feeling.

Critical thinking, creating space for debate and utilizing CBT (cognitive behaviour therapy) skills are useful ways to assess our feelings and thoughts and reframe the ones that are not useful.

Building safe spaces

Community can look like many things. For some it might be the classic friendship groups from school, university, parent groups, religious institutions or workplaces.

All of these elements may make up the places where you can share meaningful elements and may naturally show up in your day-to-day life. For many of us, in a globalized world, our communities may be more digital. Community may be less about groups and more about one-to-one relationships; it might be just a few people or it might be many. I always say if you have two to five people in your life who you can share meaningfully with you will be in a great place for boosting wellbeing.

Who are your two to five people? If you don't have that many, how can you nurture one relationship to help it become more meaningful?

Getting started

FOLLOW YOUR INTERESTS

In my experience, very few people know what they actually want so no wonder they keep feeling a bit lost. If we don't reflect and ask ourselves what matters to us then we will just get sucked into whatever is in front of us – the digital vortex being one of them.

In his book *Be Useful*, Arnold Schwarzenegger talks about having a vision for your life. He says, 'If you don't have a vision or a goal of where you're going, you drift around and you never end up anywhere.' Could it be that the reason so many people are floating around feeling burnt out, depressed and anxious is simply because they have no vision for their lives, no fulfilment and meaning?

We change over time and the things that used to light us up may not reflect who we are now. So embrace the experimentation, being a beginner and trying new things. Not only is this great for keeping our brain agile, it allows us to connect in new ways. This could be attending events, groups, courses, learning to disrupt your personal algorithm and challenge your thinking – you may even find you have fun along the way.

FIND MEANING

Make meaning your number one project. This doesn't have to be a huge philanthropic or personal achievement – meaning can be deeply personal and is about you. What makes you fulfilled, purposeful and happy? If you're not sure then experiment, reflect and iterate. That's the way all the best progress is made!

Meaning can be a conversation, staring at a tree, helping people around you. What is meaningful to you?

FIND OPPORTUNITIES FOR CONNECTION

Opportunities for meaningful connection are everywhere. We interact with people every single day; the opportunity is all around us and yet we're all wandering around lonely, waiting for someone else to make the first move.

I'm not saying you need to jump in emotionally naked with everyone, of course not. Trust is built slowly. Resilience is built through practice. Practice being brave with just one person and build up from there.

BUILD YOUR COMMUNICATION SKILLS

Effective communication is an essential skill if we're to boost connection and meaning in the digital landscape and in real life. Communication can include effective emoji use, yes, but mostly it's challenging assumptions, using collaborative language and owning our own stuff so as not to project our pain onto others but instead effectively ask for what we need and create safe spaces.

It's being fair, diplomatic and using language that is welcoming and honest. Have you ever been in a situation where you tried to communicate but your message just didn't seem to land with the other person? You just don't understand why they didn't get it. Perhaps a starting point is thinking about your own communication style. Are you hinting at what you need or being clear? Are you taking responsibility for yourself or blaming someone else for making you feel a certain way?

Summary

Thriving in a digital age is not about putting our head in the sand, denying change or spending our time complaining and essentially becoming part of the problem – it's taking responsibility for who we are in relation to the world and educating ourselves on what will boost our wellbeing overall. This includes developing the skills of empathy and communication, assessing and building communities of meaningful connection and finding personal meaning in our lives.

Now that you know what good looks like, you've gathered feedback from others and want to experiment with meaning and connection, we need to create space for these pursuits. I'm just so busy, you might say, and it's all well and good knowing what you want but there's simply not enough hours in the day.

Well, let's create space. When we focus our attention on what we really want it's important to create boundaries against the distractions. Even good things must sometimes be pushed down the list of priorities in favour of what is great. Creating boundaries is a skill that combines intention, communication and consistency and so few people have ever asked themselves – what is a healthy boundary? What do I need to say no to in order to say yes to what really matters?

CHAPTER SEVEN

Create your tech boundaries

People nod their head when I use the word boundaries, like they know exactly what I mean. But when I ask the question, 'Who knows how to set a healthy boundary and change their habits?' very few people will say yes. Instead, they talk about slipping into poor habits without meaning to, or how infuriated they become with themselves for not sticking to intentions for healthy digital use and therefore being able to do the things they really want to do.

Assess your ability to set boundaries

To see where you stand when it comes to boundaries, and whether you need better habits around them, there are some questions you can ask yourself:

- Do you often look at your day and wonder where time went?

- Do you talk about being busy but wonder what you did all day?
- Are you exhausted but unsure if you have anything to show for it?
- Do you get sucked into swiping, shopping, searching and scrolling only to find your soul feels empty and you're wondering if there's a different way to live? Is your workload an issue?
- Do you feel like the intense pressure of your job, meetings and the fear of restructures has you working all the hours to impress a boss you despise and find yourself doing emails on a beach on the vacation you finally booked with your family?

Types of boundaries

There are two types of boundaries we'll focus on: relational boundaries and digital boundaries. The principles for how you set and stick to them are broadly the same but it's useful to define where we need to set them first.

Dr Brene Brown (2018) describes a relational boundary as 'a roadmap for interactions and behaviours that we find acceptable or unacceptable'. This might include a boundary we need with a person such as a boss, partner or friend. It might also include the communication we need to do at work to challenge meeting culture or other inefficiencies that would enable us to reboot our focus and thrive.

A digital boundary is about personal limits or guidelines for managing use of digital services, online platforms and technology. This could include gaming, social media,

WhatsApp messaging, news notifications, online shopping, YouTube scrolling, Netflix binging and anything else that keeps you on your device in a way that is robbing you of meaning, focus and a sense of wellbeing.

How do you know you need a boundary?

Resentment. Feeling resentment is known as the early sign of needing to set a boundary. We begin to resent the person or environment for taking up our time or that we're doing something we really don't want to do. When it comes to relational boundaries, we often forget that other people in our lives are not aware of the vision we've created for our life and are just doing what they do – they don't know that there is a negative impact on our health or focus. Resentment is an initial clue that gives us information; it tells us we need a boundary to protect our time, emotions, focus or resources. Once we recognize this feeling for what it is, we then need space to consider what boundary we need and, crucially, how to communicate it effectively so we're more likely to reap the benefits.

We often skip this last step and then become frustrated that our boundary is not respected – but we never told anyone about it.

When it comes to digital boundaries, you will probably already know if you need one. You may wake up exhausted because you stayed up late doing something pointless online, you may work on holidays or find it hard to relax even if you do have time off, and you may feel lonely, restless, irritable or frazzled. Your habits may be negatively impacted, such as your health, meaningful connections or finances. We are wise to set boundaries early on rather than wait for the extremes of addiction to set in, but with the fast pace of digital change it can be difficult to just have a fixed boundary that stays static from now until forever. Your boundaries might be just fine until you're exhausted, upset or triggered and then suddenly it seems they fly out the window.

Another clue that you need to review your boundaries is your mental health. Are you experiencing low mood, depression, anxiety or burnout? Are you wondering if it's really to do with work or your digital health overall: meeting culture, negative news, being always on, distraction, addiction, information overload?

If any of these feel true for you and you've assessed where you're at in life, it's time to think about the boundaries that are personal to you that you want to set.

But first, a reminder to ask yourself what good looks like in your boundary setting. This starts with creating a vision for your life.

How to create a vision for your life

If we are going to build new habits, we need to focus on what we DO want, not just what we want less of. This may seem counterintuitive when talking about boundaries and refocusing your attention, but it's based on positive psychology.

Boundaries are tactics but what are you actually protecting? It can help us stick to boundaries if we know what they are protecting – our time, resources and energy.

The vision for your life doesn't have to be like Arnold Schwarzenegger's big dreams of becoming Mr Universe, a leading man in movies and living in America. Those were his dreams. Your vision might be to support your family, to create a loving home or break generational trauma patterns passed on to you. Your vision might be about contentment, love, giving back, fulfilment or achieving your fullest potential.

I've never had a fixed five-year plan. Some people swear by them – they know exactly where they're headed and set clear goals and how to achieve them. Personally, I think this approach can sometimes limit the magic of life – you don't know what you don't know so predicting how it's going to go and trying to doggedly stick to it can take away from the flow of adaptation to change and new opportunities. Everyone is different and that's ok.

Your vision doesn't have to be clear, it doesn't have to go on a vision board and it doesn't have to have a perfect formula of goals. Your vision can be filled with what you don't want. I'm never going back there! I know there is a different way! It's a belief maybe, a gentle knowing, a commitment to yourself and a North Star that just feels right to you.

Write down the vision for your life. It can be messy and incomplete, and it will definitely evolve, but get your why down on paper and then the tactics for boundaries will be easier to identify and execute.

Identify and practise

Now map out what boundaries you think you need. Your boundaries are the tactics that will give you the space to put in the work to achieve the vision for your life. They'll give you insights into where you need to say no so that you have the space to say yes to what really matters.

They should be a living, breathing agreement with yourself that will evolve over time depending on factors such as goals, work projects, emotional state and your feeling of community and overall wellbeing. It's essential that you create space for dreaming and reflection in your life so that you can tune into the data your body sends you and understand what you need at different times in your life.

Once you identify a boundary that you want to start with, communicate that boundary to those who will be directly affected and then be kind to yourself as you practice. Setting a new boundary is like setting any new habit. It takes time to create new habits but 'habits you repeat daily largely determine your health, wealth and happiness', according to James Clear in his bestselling book *Atomic Habits*.

A word on addiction and boundaries

In my research for this book, I spoke with experts and laypeople. There was one conversation in particular that captured the nuance when it comes to compulsion versus addiction and why simply setting a tactical boundary can be so hard for some.

A successful male in his late 40s who was recently single, said:

> You know, Petra, even if I delete the social apps and set the intention, I'll just go the long way to access the info through my browser. It doesn't stop me. I'm in a constant battle of checking things even if I know there won't be any messages. This includes emails outside of work, social apps I've deleted and if I'm sitting alone… I'll go through my phone and text people to meet up that I don't even like. I'll then be sitting there for a coffee with them, eventually thinking, 'I don't even like you or want to hang out – I just couldn't sit with myself three nights ago and now here I am'.

As he spoke, I related to so much of what he said. People don't talk about the quiet moments when we know all the tactics around boundaries and yet, there we are doing the same thing again because it's just easy, it's just habit.

You may not resonate with this extreme, you may be the person who thinks, 'well, just manage your device' – the one who thinks it's not the device's fault, it's a you problem. But it might resonate with those of you who move up and down the continuum of addiction. Sometimes you can set the intention, delete the apps and then suddenly, it seems, there you are again, losing time on something you didn't intend. Wondering where you'll find the time or energy to live out the vision for your life.

I think we'd all agree that devices are set up to keep our attention and we're all at risk of compulsion, which can be triggered by a few key things:

- If we're of an older generation, technology and the habit around it might have less of a hold in our brain's neural pathways.

- If we're in a vulnerable place in life, we may be more susceptible to these distractions as we're more inclined to numb our emotions and seek out the happy dopamine hormone if we're stressed, sad or in pain.
- If we're genetically predisposed to addictive behaviours in a more extreme sense then technology (gaming, pornography, gambling, scrolling, shopping) may just be the flavour of the time – an obsession that allows us to avoid how we feel.

It's my belief that addiction affects us all. It's my friend who wakes up and loses an hour scrolling through the news and LinkedIn articles and it's the guy sitting alone going through three steps to get to his emails even though it's a Sunday and he knows there's nothing important coming through.

Be honest

This is why thriving in a digital world takes radical honesty. Only you know the full extent of the pull it has on you, so the first step is radical honesty and a healthy dose of self-compassion. When it comes to boundaries, you may have all the tactics in the world and yet still find yourself stuck and feeling ashamed that you just can't stick to them.

Knowing the machine is set up to keep us there can help us with self-compassion and a realization that we may need an honest community to help us live differently. This is the main power of any type of addiction recovery group – being honest with others.

The trick is to find your honesty tribe. This can be one person or more, it can be someone you live with or a work colleague – the steps for setting boundaries will still apply, it may just feel a bit like a roller coaster at first as you work towards finding your equilibrium and, crucially, keeping your why in placc. There is a full and rich life that will be missed if you're hiding out, whatever that looks like to you.

The digital detox

There are different views on the topic of digital detox. Some people swear by them as a useful reset and others, like Johann Hari in his book *Stolen Focus*, highlight the ineffectiveness of this approach as it doesn't solve the business model that is putting billions of dollars into competing for our attention. It's true that a personal digital detox won't solve the systemic issues in the way technology is set up or set the boundaries necessary to live alongside technology in our day-to-day lives.

I nodded along in agreement with Hari when reading his book and yet not long ago I experienced a five-day unintentional digital detox that was so refreshing and insightful that I decided there was more to it than I initially thought. Granted it didn't solve the full picture of my day-to-day addiction to tech, but it did offer me help.

I had viewed the detox as something uniquely available to the privileged few who – able to unplug from everything with no worries about work, finances or dependents – could float off into a retreat in Bali, meditating and unplugging from all the annoying responsibilities of life. I realized a digital dctox can actually be much simpler than that and can act as a reset in our daily lives.

Recently I had an opportunity to visit Jordan, a beautifully rich country of culture and history. While there I visited the desert of Wadi Rum and spent an evening with no light pollution, staring at the stars with absolutely no connection to the outside world. My phone simply wouldn't work in the middle of the desert.

I felt the same level of resourcing as you might get from a three-day health detox. A fast or cleanse can do a great job of resetting your gut, helping you withdraw from sugar and processed food addictions and allowing space for reflection on habits. It doesn't solve the accessibility of processed foods, the obesity epidemic or how our sedentary and easy lifestyles make it easier to be unhealthy, but it is a great way to intermittently check in on your physical health and clean up your insides.

The first day of a sugar and caffeine detox can feel horrific as you withdraw, but by day three you feel superhuman – energetic and ready to take on the world. Yes, within a few weeks you're likely to slip into those caffeine and sugar habits again but that doesn't negate the health benefits and it acts as an opportunity to reflect on negative habits so that you can get up and try again.

Day one of a digital detox can feel like something's missing, there's a phantom phone in our hand and we don't quite know what to do with our thumbs. If we attempt a detox in our usual environment, something like standing in a queue will take immense focus to not reach for our device while waiting. To sit in the discomfort of your own skin instead of multitasking feels unnatural, which is why a digital detox is usually done as part of a trip away from our work and usual distractions and triggers – our phone away from our pocket so that we are forced to find other ways of coping with quiet.

Space to stare into nature, have no pressure, sleep and level out our nervous system is a great way to keep our device turned off and ignore the pressures of the world around us. We might say that it's the combination of factors that enables us to reset, reminding ourselves what truly matters as we breathe again, read an actual book and perhaps feel the soil or sand on our feet.

We then want to make that feeling last as long as possible, so a thought about reintegration into your life will not prevent the pull of addiction fully, but it will boost your intention for who you want to be and perhaps reconnect you to the vision of your life.

While the digital detox is definitely not the solution to the bigger tech challenges we are facing systemically, a detox can kickstart your resolve at embedding fresh boundaries by giving you actual space to reflect on who you are, what you want and what boundaries might help you navigate the fast-paced world we live in.

So let's set some digital boundaries

Boundaries are deeply personal and simply take full honesty and a knowledge that they will take time, failure and resets to get right. It's about using your growth mindset to understand who you are, remain compassionate for your humanity and continue to step up and work towards the vision of your life.

Here's an example of my imperfect boundaries that enable me to create space to invest in the vision for my life:

- I turn off all notifications and remove social media apps from my phone. This means I can be more intentional about when I access social media.
- I turn off noises, pings and most sounds from my desktop, laptop and phone. Sounds trigger my nervous system in a way that affects my survival fight or flight response, so I am careful to have pleasant sounds on my alarm and WhatsApp and everything else like Slack or email switched off.
- I rarely watch the news – and I definitely do not have a news app or notifications of any kind on my laptop, desktop or phone. I protect myself from clickbait and negative news by only accessing news on my own timetable from validated sources. You may find this is too extreme but for me it's essential.
- I prioritize connection and movement so that my life is rich, full and fulfilling. This might mean spending time researching events that bring me joy online but making sure I show up IRL.
- I try to consciously leave my phone in a bag or pocket when out with friends. I've actually learned this one the hard way by asking for feedback from my friends who highlighted that my phone was slipping into my relationships in a way that made them feel devalued. I have to keep revisiting this boundary as it tends to slip if I'm not careful.
- I will often leave my phone at least a metre away from me when I'm with family members. This seems like a

silly tactic to some but remember I'm on the addiction end of the continuum, so I need to take drastic measures to curb my digital usage in order to stay present with people I love.
- I create regular space for reflection by journaling or walking where I can remind myself of what matters, the vision for my life and then revisit the boundaries that are in my control in a world of change and uncertainty.

These boundaries are personal to me and not a one-size-fits-all, but they may help you begin to think about the digital boundaries you need to begin or revisit.

Ask yourself, what boundaries do I want to set or remind myself of in order to invest in the vision for my life?

List three here that you'd like to practise:

1 ………………………………………………………………..

2 ………………………………………………………………...

3 ………………………………………………………………..

While this book is about digital wellbeing it can also be useful to think of your relational boundaries here – who are the people that you need boundaries with in order to protect your wellbeing? Maybe you have a friend who's been struggling and taking up a lot of your emotional bandwidth. If you're beginning to feel resentful it can be useful to think about what type of emotional boundary you need so that you have space to invest in your own wellbeing.

Communicate your boundaries to those affected

There was a great quote I learned when training to be a coach with the Coach Training Institute (CTI), which said, 'People are creative, resourceful and whole'. Think about that for a moment. So often we are trying to fix people but this quote serves as a useful reminder that while it's important to be there for others, it's also important to communicate boundaries.

We may fear we're letting people down when we stick to our own digital and relational boundaries, but actually we may be a valuable example of what it takes to boost our focus and wellbeing and create a ripple effect of change.

Digital and relational boundaries can cross over. When we're putting in place a digital boundary, we may need to communicate this boundary to the people who will be affected. This is a crucial step that is often missed and then we get frustrated that we can't stick to the boundary – but we didn't tell the people and so they pushed back in some way. Why didn't you answer the email, pick up the phone etc? Which can make us defensive or feel like giving up on the boundaries we're trying to set.

Instead, we might proactively communicate our boundaries to those who will be affected. We might tell our team if we're off emails for a few hours while we're focusing on a project and offer a way that they can still reach us in an emergency. We might tell a partner that we're leaving our phone off when out with a friend so they understand we're trying to be present, or we might let a friend know that we're taking a few days of digital detox but would love to have a call and connect at a later date.

It can take vulnerability to talk about our boundaries openly as we may think it makes us look like we have poor willpower or are somehow flawed and so we struggle in silence. Bringing our boundary challenges into the light helps us realize we are not alone and rather than all having a pity party about how the machine is set up against us (which yes it mostly is), we can create positive accountability where we can support each other to stick to boundaries and ask each other questions about the vision for our lives.

Reflection prompts

Having that digital detox can be a great way to gain some distance from your situation so you can map out effective boundaries. Sometimes when we're in the day-to-day struggle and our nervous system is firefighting it can be difficult to zoom out and see what we really need. We just want to feel less frazzled but aren't quite sure where to start with tackling this feeling.

Here are some additional reflective questions that could inform a digital detox or reflection period:

- What have I learned from feedback about my relationship to technology?
- What's making me feel frazzled and what is in my control to change?
- Where do I feel resentment and what kind of boundaries would help – relational, digital or a combination of both?
- Who do I need to communicate my boundaries to in order to have them respected?

Accountability and support

When returning from a digital detox or taking a little time to reflect and create some intentional boundaries it can be useful to find an accountability buddy. I mean, not just find one off the street, but think about a friend, partner or colleague who also wants some accountability and do a skills trade. Let them know what you're working on and what you want to be kept accountable for and ask if you can repay the favour – if there's anything they want to be kept accountable for – and create a plan to check in on each other.

You can also hire a coach who, let's face it, will help you work on mindset but is also a glorified accountability buddy – someone who will help you map out your values and vision for life as well as set goals and check in on your progress. So if this is something you can afford, it can be a useful space away from your day-to-day struggles to reflect with an objective outsider who can challenge your thinking and help you stay accountable.

You don't have to pay for a coach, though. We live in an age where we can learn from mentors all over the world, from their experiences on mindset and goalsetting, but it's the accountability that can be hard to come by if we don't set it up ourselves.

If you want digital wellbeing it's essential to take some ownership of the vision for your life, intentions and boundaries and then elicit community and support to help you along your way.

With the foundations in place, let's remind ourselves of the joy of living and how focusing our intention on what matters can recharge our focus and reboot our life.

CHAPTER EIGHT

Find your focus and reclaim your joy

We have been conditioned to believe that we need a reason for joy, a motivation to feel gratitude, grounds to be in a state of love DR JOE DISPENZA

Reclaiming joy is about finding balance, connecting with what matters most to you, and nurturing your physical, emotional and mental health. It involves being intentional about your choices and actions, and sometimes it requires seeking support from others. By incorporating these strategies into your life, you can create a foundation for sustained joy and fulfilment.

Moments of joy can surprise us at times – a breeze in the sunshine, a great view, seeing a toddler take their first steps or connecting deeply with a friend. Life is filled with moments of poignancy, pain and sadness but also joy and love. If we want to fully engage with what it means to be human, it helps to nurture the skill of openness, so we can notice the joy that shows up every day.

When this feels hard it's useful to be reminded that we can also cultivate joy over time. The goal of life is not to feel happy or joyful every second of the day – this isn't realistic and, if anything, the tough times help us appreciate the joyful times more – but we can create the conditions that enable joy and happiness to happen more frequently, and importantly, to be savoured when they do show up.

In our fast-paced societies fuelled by tech efficiencies, we can easily fill up all the space with things to do, check or focus on, forgetting that it's in the mind-wandering that we remember what truly matters, enabling us to find focus on the right things.

Finding our focus can be about a work project but if we zoom out on our whole lives it's removing the distractions and stressors that prevent us from focusing on what we will really value and cherish on our deathbed many years from now.

How to cultivate joy

So how do we cultivate joy?

It's about protecting our mind from negative influences and proactively adding positive influences. This doesn't mean keeping our head in the sand about world events, but it does mean vigorously guarding our brain, the energy we give to certain thoughts and, rather than just turning down the volume on some things, making sure we're also filling up the deficit with joyful thoughts and experiences.

Deciding how we want to think and experience life is crucial to cultivating joy.

As Victor Frankl stated in his best-selling book *Man's Search for Meaning* (1946), where he reflects on his experience in Auschwitz, 'Everything can be taken from a man except one thing, the last of the human freedoms – to choose one's attitude in any given circumstance. To choose one's own way.'

This is a powerful quote as it highlights that this isn't all about our environments or surroundings, but instead it's about the meaning we give things, it's about which thoughts we choose to believe and how we cultivate our response to the changing world around us.

Here are some ways to get started, small things that when put together enable us to reduce the negative impacts of technology and create more intention around how we think for ourselves and nurture the environments to help us focus and thrive.

Practice gratitude

People who express gratitude regularly can see great benefits to both their physical and mental health, with a 2012 study highlighting the benefits for relationships too (Bartlett et al, 2012). I can personally attest to the benefit of focusing my attention on gratitude; it was one of the first small practices that enabled me to rewire my thinking, writing down three things I was grateful for each day for months. It was a crucial practice for moving me from a victim mindset to a growth mindset. Here are two ways you can set up a gratitude practice.

Keep a gratitude journal: simply writing down small things you're thankful for can help you shift your mindset to one of opportunity rather than defeat.

Express your appreciation: we're very quick to express judgement these days and yet it can feel awkward or vulnerable to say out loud what we appreciate or love about what somebody does or who they are as a person.

Communicating our gratitude for others is a crucial part of building community and connection and something each of us can start today.

Engage in activities you love

Proactively putting yourself in environments where you feel good and thrive feels like a no-brainer and yet so often life gets in the way. I joined an intense gym class once and welcomed the new guy whose first day it was; he was quick to say it had been four years since he'd come to this class that he loved, probably as a way to excuse his lack of fitness. I asked him what had kept him from the class if he loved it so much and he said, 'Oh, you know, work'.

See where you might match this thinking with anything that you do. What have you given up that you love because daily responsibilities have gotten in the way? You may not have the resources to dive in fully now but there may be a small way you can integrate that thing into your life if you get creative and prioritize. If not now, it may inform your why, the reason you get up and strive for greater space or security in the future.

Foster healthy relationships

Toxic relationship cycles can be one of the most draining elements in life and can suck out the joy of our day-to-day existence. People forget, however, that if you have a growth mindset and can challenge Disney-style assumptions about how relationships go, you'll realize that relationships and communication in relationships are crucial skills that can be developed.

Check out the books, articles and podcasts by renowned relationship expert Esther Perel if you want to get started in developing this skill.

Take care of your physical health

Everyone is different and different things will work at different times, but I know for me, if I do a high-intensity workout, I immediately feel joy and happy dopamine hormones floating through me. It's immediate and invigorating as it helps to build momentum for healthy habits and enhances my ability to focus on projects I love.

Part of the digital wellbeing issue is how sedentary we are. We move from our bed to our car to our desk to our sofa to our bed. We need to be intentional about including movement into our day if we want the natural highs we so often seek in fake form through our devices. Physical activity releases endorphins which improve mood, resilience and focus. Eating nutritious food and getting enough sleep also help give us the resilient foundations to make joy more possible.

Ask yourself, what are the health habits you want to cultivate and how will progress in this area support the vision for your life alongside the boundaries you need to set to help you get there?

Mindfulness and meditation

There is plenty of information in the world about mindfulness and meditation and its purpose in essence to help us stay in the present moment – the only place where life really happens.

The theory is that it's in the present that we feel joy; however, we spend a lot of our time focused on worrying about the past or the future. Cultivating our ability to be right here, right now means that we will feel a range of human emotions, including pain and sorrow but also joy, happiness and fulfilment. Do you want to numb out the good experiences because you're so busy armouring up against the possible negatives? That's no way to live.

You may be able to focus on your breath or you may have tried a meditation app or other form of exercise to help you stay present but even if none of that works for you or the habit has slipped away – that's ok. You can be mindful simply by getting connected to your senses.

What can you see around you, what do you hear, what can you feel, smell or taste? Connecting to our senses is the quickest way to bring us right into the present. If I am triggered by something due to my complex PTSD, I remind myself to wiggle my toes, and this brings me back to right here. So simple when you think about it. It's simply connecting back to our body.

This may seem silly and not something that's part of a three-step hack for mindfulness, but it does the trick for me. The point is, experiment with what works for you, whether it's a more formal meditation practice or simply pinching yourself and realizing how lucky you are simply to breathe another breath and live in your unique skin. It's funny how it often takes a close friend falling ill or a near-death experience for us to embrace this perspective.

Limit negative influences and cultivate a positive mindset

We've discussed boundaries and turning down the noise on negativity in your life. If you want to cultivate joy, you'll also develop the skill of reframing your thoughts and deciding what meaning you give them.

I'll say something bold here: sometimes therapy doesn't actually help with this. I know, I know, sacrilege! You may have thought that the current advice is that therapy is always good for everyone! Well, to be honest, not always. Sometimes we go to therapy and feel worse and sure, sometimes this is because we're uncovering some deep things that have been hidden for a long time but at other times it's simply because we keep regurgitating our worries and fears without reframing these thoughts into something useful.

A friend of mine lives with depression. He told me he's been in therapy for a few years and then shared with me some of the music he listens to. His music was so deeply melancholic that I had to switch it off as I knew that for me, if I listened to that kind of music all the time it would negatively affect my mood. Everyone is different so this doesn't mean he shouldn't listen to it as he finds beauty in the melancholic but, for me, it's not something my brain can engage in often without staying stuck there. So in the same way, would talking about problems for an hour a week with no recourse for reframing or taking action on what's in my control be the solution for me? At some points it has been; these days, less so.

I'm all for listening to some sappy love songs after a heartbreak to help with the necessary grieving and to feel all the feels but there comes a time when we need to decide to no longer listen to those songs but instead move into more uplifting beats and have a change of scene – to put our brain and body in the environment that we want more of.

Mindset is deeply personal, as the only one who knows what's going on is us. So if you find yourself in a thinking loop that's bringing you down, practise that creative growth mindset and get on a quest to decide if there are other ways you can think about the issue or, even more radical, whether you can let go of it completely.

Give back and practise kindness

Volunteering or engaging in random acts of kindness is crucial to cultivating joy. This can be in small ways, like offering a listening ear to a friend, or in bigger ways, like committing to a volunteering opportunity in your area.

When I went through my breakup and lived on my own, yes I spent a bit of time with the sad love songs, cried it out and then got up and tried to find out where I could give back in some small way. I found a project in my local area where I simply needed to help in the kitchen. No big decisions, no status, just getting to know the other volunteers and getting stuck into practical work. I remember one day sitting on the top deck of a bus crying as I felt the deep pain of grief, and by the time I'd finished volunteering I had made a complete turnaround, feeling joy and hope.

Giving back got me out of my head and my small-world problems and gave me perspective. Perspective is a beautiful thing. It's about embracing our humanity, not minimizing our struggle but also connecting us into the wider universe of energy and possibility.

What are the ways you cultivate joy? If you're not sure because it's been so long, try to think back to the last time you felt joy. What was happening, what were the conditions, who was you with, where were you? Go in your past for clues and then cultivate the conditions as mentioned above to help you re-experience the joys of life.

What's all the fuss about focus?

Boundaries, joy, a vision for your life, listening to your body and acknowledging your digital distractions are all part of the conversation about focus. When we know where we're headed there's a purpose to our focus time and we can feel more in flow doing meaningful work that gives us a sense of achievement.

In an age where digital distractions are ubiquitous, cultivating digital focus is essential for productivity, mental wellbeing and overall effectiveness. By implementing strategies to manage distractions, create structured routines and leverage technology wisely, you can enhance your ability to maintain focus in a digital world.

There are many productivity tools and hacks that all stem from one concept – finding flow. There are many apps and tools that essentially help to block out time without digital distraction in order to get into a flow state where our highest productivity shows up. The concept of flow, made popular by Mihaly Csikszentmihalyi in his book *Finding Flow* (1998), means complete immersion into an activity that leads to high productivity and satisfaction. Some of the ways you know you're in flow include intense focus, clear goals, balance between challenge and skills and a loss of self-consciousness due to being so immersed – even altering your perception of time. You're doing something so interesting, almost obsessively, that you look up and go, wow has that much time passed, I had no idea.

I realize we're not going to achieve a full flow state every day and with every work project we do but it's a useful state to cultivate – even if it's during a hobby or in conversation with great people. We can create the conditions that will enable us to achieve this state more often because in my mind, achieving these states is intrinsic to finding those states of joy too.

Cultivating a flow state

Mihaly includes some of the following conditions to help achieve a flow state:

- For flow to occur, tasks must be challenging enough to engage and motivate but not so difficult that they cause anxiety or frustration.
- Continuously improving skills to match the increasing challenges of tasks ensures sustained engagement and productivity.
- Clearly defined goals provide direction and purpose, making it easier to focus and work efficiently.

- Feedback is important. Receiving immediate feedback on performance helps individuals adjust their actions and stay on track, while the ability to self-assess and make corrections fosters a sense of autonomy, competence and fulfilment.
- Creating an environment that minimizes distraction and encourages concentration enhances the quality of work and sense of achievement, with time management techniques being valuable for some.

Ask yourself, when it comes to focus, what is in your control? Is your work either at home or in the office conducive for flow states? Is there anything in your control that could enable you to feel a flow state more often? If your answer is 'no' when it comes to the workplace, it might be time to ask questions to see what can change to match you to a better role where your skills can flourish. Or perhaps it's time to think about a bigger change that can boost your wellbeing overall.

Learning focus in an age of digital distraction takes radical honesty, accountability and a clear why – if these tactics don't seem to work, you might be focusing on what someone else wants you to do and your body is slowly rebelling.

A little tough love – snowflakes, resilience and thriving

I love listening to motivation videos on YouTube with the likes of David Goggins, Arnold Schwarzenegger, Eric

Thomas aka The Hip Hop Preacher and others who are a bit shouty, direct and treat life like a military exercise. They say things like get up when you're feeling down, discipline trumps motivation every time and no one is coming to save you.

This is not everyone's cup of self-love tea but for me it slaps me out of my pity party and reminds me that I am responsible for my own life. It reminds me to get up and do the work – and I love it!

Wellbeing is not all about bubble baths and candles, it's not all about duvet days and feeling our feelings – sometimes it's about getting up despite how you feel, having the hard conversations, challenging the natural pull of laziness, switching off distractions, showing up at the gym, failing hard, being vulnerable and showing up again and again.

Resilience is our capacity to withstand or recover quickly from difficulties. It's toughness. It includes elasticity and an ability to bounce back and keep going.

While resilience is sometimes weaponized as something people *should* do when they are in toxic or controlling environments and this is not ok, the core of resilience is intrinsic to wellbeing and learning to thrive amidst the immense change we are seeing in the world today.

My question to you is where is your mental toughness?

Do you want to hear that life is hard and you should accept the system, the greed and powers that be and go have a duvet day and talk about your problems for the next few years at great expense to yourself? Or should you get up, dust yourself off once again and fight for joy, love and humanity?

We've all had our resilience tested over the last few years and it's likely it will continue to be tested. We might use the negative phrasing 'snowflake generation' to criticize Gen Z and their perceived lack of resilience and emotional sensitivity and while there are definitely some generational differences that impact perceptions and values between generations, we all need a little tough love from time to time no matter which generation we're in.

We need to wake up to our one short life and ask ourselves how we want to live. Do we want to sit indoors scrolling and numbing or do we want to be experiencing and living? This doesn't need to be big bucket-list things, it's about living our authentic life, whatever that is for us.

The Five Regrets of the Dying

There's a great book called *The Five Regrets of the Dying* (2019), a memoir by a woman called Bonnie Ware who worked in palliative care. In her years of supporting those at the end she discovered five key regrets that show up again and again and I'll list them here for your reflection.

These are the most common wishes of the dying:

1 I wish I'd had the courage to live a life true to myself, not the life others expected of me.
2 I wish I hadn't worked so hard.
3 I wish I'd had the courage to express my feelings.
4 I wish I'd stayed in touch with my friends.
5 I wish I had let myself be happier.

Read those again! What jumps out at you? What makes you pause and think, of course, I wish those things already, but I'm scared, I'm waiting for the right time, I'm busy achieving, I'm busy at work.

My tough love for you today is a reminder to ask yourself the big questions. Questions to get you off the path that has been laid out for you by someone else and instead to challenge you to forge your own path.

These five things are not static. Sometimes we think that it's finding that happy moment, arriving at that destination and then we're good, but it's the awareness that these things matter and then it's the relentless pursuit of them, evolving over time. Just as our bodies need stress to build muscle, so maintaining great friendships, for example, needs effort. People evolve and so great connections need self-awareness, an ability to admit mistakes, vulnerability, humility and an investment of time. It's easier to get hurt at the first hurdle and back off into a sea of shallow connections and rationalize that the friendship faded because of the other person – but ask yourself, what's on me?

Progress, not perfection

Global speaker and coach Tony Robbins, who has worked with hundreds of thousands of people, believes that 'progress equals happiness. Even if you're not where you want to be yet'. He says, 'If you're on the road, if you're improving, if you're making progress, you're going to love it. You're going to feel alive' (2022).

We get very obsessed with the destination in many societies. When we achieve our education we'll be happy, when we get that big job, when we get married, when we have kids or buy a house and on and on the list goes. What happens though is our expectations of how long that feeling of achievement will last are very different from the reality and so we question ourselves. Why isn't this enough, why don't I feel great now, why doesn't this feeling last, why do I feel like I'm just on the bottom rung of a whole new ladder, why don't I feel happy?

Well maybe there's something in Tony Robbins' idea about progress. This whole concept is captured in the popular true story of Chris Gardner in the 2006 movie *The Pursuit of Happyness*. The title says it right there, the notion taken from the American Declaration of Independence that 'all men are created equal, that they are endowed by their creator with certain unalienable rights, that among these are life, liberty and the *pursuit* of happiness.' There's something in the journey, the effort and the movement that must be considered when thinking about our wellbeing, something about the process of living this life, not just the destination, which of course, for everyone, is death.

We can cultivate joy and happiness for sure, but it's not about sitting on a mountain for 24 hours a day taking in the view – what makes the mountainous view great is the climb. There's a different feeling when you see a photograph of a view from the top than when you've climbed to the top yourself; there's something in the effort it took to get there and the connection to something greater than yourself, to something bigger than you.

The question remains, what are you pursuing and to what end? Is it your agenda or someone else's?

As Chris Gardner, played by Will Smith, says to his son in that iconic scene, 'Don't ever let someone tell you that you can't do something. Not even me. You got a dream, you gotta protect it. When people can't do something themselves, they're gonna tell you that you can't do it. You want something, go get it.'

When people talk about wellbeing they often say you should slow down. Reduce your dreams, just accept a simple life or their version of what wellness looks like. I'm saying listen to you and only you. Don't pursue someone else's dream for your life, don't think that optimum wellbeing and joy look the same for everyone.

If your soul is the soul of an athlete, then pursue that goal relentlessly.

If your heart is the heart of an academic, then push for the research and work that matters to you.

If your joy is raising children and creating a safe place, go and do that.

If your spirit is calling you to travel like a nomad and never put down roots, please pursue this life.

I could go on and on to list the many ways we could listen to who we are and fan that flame of our unique presence in the world, but the crucial point is, is it your life or someone else's?

Within our pursuit there will be times when we sacrifice. We'll sacrifice social life or health, we'll push ourselves to achieve, and we'll swing to one end of the pendulum and then the other before finding our middle ground, whatever work-life balance means to us.

Some people love their work; it's a vocation and holds meaning and I don't think we should shame that. Work-life balance does not look the same for each of us. It's about creating your unique version of work-life harmony and recognizing your whole self, the person who will one day be on their death bed asking, did I live a good life, did I live *my* life?

Was I authentic and honest about my feelings, did I say what I meant and love deeply or was I afraid? Did I lose years of my life on social media or in shallow connection or did I step into the deep waters of joy and love, knowing full well that this would also mean I'd experience pain and sorrow in my full and rich life too?

Action steps

Only you can answer the above reflective questions.

If you're truly honest with yourself the answers to these questions may require some change in how you live your life. They may require some bravery, an adjustment to your approach, some honesty with yourself and others – this too is a pursuit, a journey of learning to be honest with ourselves and of elasticity as we fall, feel vulnerable, mess up and then pick ourselves up again to pursue the things that feed our soul and allow us to fully feel alive.

What are the top three things you want to start with so that you can once again experiment with what lights you up and brings you joy?

Conclusion

I started this book somewhat overwhelmed by the enormity of this topic and I have to say, I'm left with the same feeling. I would be lying if, as an addict, I told you these insights and tactics, while true and useful, feel like the whole solution.

There are times when life feels smooth, relationships are easy and I sit in a place where the world makes sense, and I can make great cognitive choices like 'have boundaries' and 'prioritize community' and the healthy things that help me thrive.

In recent times, however, going through my personal dark night of the soul, it's a much harder cycle. People offer advice about my life and the guilt I feel at some of my choices; they say you should learn to sit with yourself, you should be alone, you should learn to breathe, to meditate, to not date, to date better, to work out in this way or fill your soul with these things – then this time will go quicker, you'll feel better and the universe will show you the way.

It's funny how everyone has the best advice for other people!

Some days all of those things work and some days I'll do the advice thing for others. I meditated for a day and felt amazing and subsequently told my immediate circle they should try it too. There's nothing wrong with giving advice, with trying things, trying to alleviate other people's pain, and as I've outlined in this book, we need conversation to bring shame into the light and to create positive accountability to navigate this world together.

But at the same time, it's crucial to be real with you. The principles in this book absolutely hold true and yet it's the consistency of putting them into practice amidst this very real world that makes us feel like we're missing out on all the wonderful things the world has to offer or that we're wrong to feel lonely or stuck, somehow pathologizing very normal human emotions as we navigate urban cities and try to put plasters on the wounds we feel will never heal.

When we're lonely we're desperate for crumbs of connection, our masks talking to other people's masks in the hopes of being seen but too scared to really go first. The levels of resilience we need to just keep up, to turn off the noise, to be ourselves in a world that celebrates fakes, to do wellbeing, to talk about it, to not talk about it, to keep a roof over our head while being authentic, to retain a relationship or home in a world of distraction, to stay upbeat when once again we were sucked into the addictive

CONCLUSION

nature of not being enough. Let's say it right here in the conclusion: it's a lot.

And yet, humans are powerfully adaptive creatures. We have survived disasters, wars and seismic changes in history with grit and resolve, managing to pull together as communities of hope and action. We are not meant to evolve alone. We need each other and we need to keep the skills of reflection, presence, resilience, empathy and authenticity at the forefront of our evolution.

What do these skills mean to you in practice?

Reflection is both a habit and a mindset. You may journal at the beginning of your day or pause throughout; you might reflect with a friend or jot down your musings on paper. Reflection is the space to turn down the volume on the noise around you and critically assess your thoughts and feelings and decide on actions that are useful for your overall life. Reflection is also tears and sadness, allowing emotion to flow, to notice and give space to pain and overwhelm. To release the pressure valve and really listen.

Presence is the skill of being right here right now. It's a practice of bringing ourselves back to where life is truly lived – not over there in the future or just when we've achieved things. It's right here, right now. Blink and you miss it. Presence is leaving our screens and connecting to someone's soul, really seeing the world around us and thanking our body for being the vehicle we get to experience life in.

We've talked a lot about resilience and like I said, you might be navigating a lot right now. You may feel that dreaded sense of overwhelm or, as a coaching client recently said to me, 'I've made my bed and now I have to lie in it', as if there was nothing else that could be done than stay stuck in misery.

Resilience holds radical honesty and pain within it. It's acknowledging how we've messed up or what we've lost; it's acceptance that life isn't exactly as we imagined and sometimes feeling that it's just too much; it's noticing all of those things and feeling them fully; it's then about getting up. Again. No matter how many times you've gotten it wrong or fallen, it's standing tall and imagining the background music that helps you rise. It's learning and taking full responsibility for who you are in the world and putting that next foot in front of the other, being brave enough to fully be here, to feel, to move, to love.

Empathy is that beautiful place of connection where we can feel with people, where we practice truly seeing others and thereby play our part in enhancing community and connection. Empathy is filled with boundaries because it makes choices to turn down the noise of everyone's problems in the whole world and instead opens up boldly to our sphere of influence – the people directly around us. This may sound radical to some but if we're going to prevent empathy fatigue we need to choose where we put our attention and how we resource ourselves.

Empathy can be practised for ourselves as well as others and must stand next to boundaries in order to protect the flame and enable it to grow – empathy is a crucial skill for leadership both at work and in our personal lives.

And finally, my favourite and most crucial skill: authenticity. This skill takes courage. It's the bravery to be seen as you are, to show up even if you'll be misunderstood, to continue to dust yourself off and be the hero in your own movie. To love, to fight, to feel and celebrate your humanity.

As Theodore Roosevelt is quoted as saying (and Dr Brene Brown has made famous):

> The credit belongs to the man who is actually in the arena, whose face is marred by dust and sweat and blood; who strives valiantly… who comes short again and again, but who does actually strive to do the deeds; who knows great enthusiasms; who spends himself in a worthy cause; who at the best knows in the end the triumph of high achievement, and who at the worst, if he fails, at least fails while daring greatly.

In the face of artificial intelligence, deep fakes, fake news and competition for our attention among all the other challenges laid out in this book, it's our shared humanity that will enable us to thrive. We need to dial this up, not down. So many of us are hiding behind our devices. We hide behind our meetings, our Slack channels, our dating apps, work pressures, social media accounts and productivity tools. We are getting used to hiding and atrophying the skills that make us human, even labelling them as illnesses or problems to be sorted, making more of us ashamed of who we are, perpetuating the cycle that makes us hide even more.

This approach is doing us a disservice. It's imperative that rather than hide or medicalize our humanity we embrace it. We open up about who we are and navigate the choppy waters of change together, our heads held high, arm in arm rather than flailing alone on a dinghy wondering why we feel like we're drowning.

While there will continue to be many hacks and three-step plans for managing our devices, boosting wellness and managing our mental health, what if it's just so much simpler than that? What if it's just about embracing who we are? Maybe it's in our messiness that we will once again find our superpowers and find joy where there is fear, connection where there is loneliness and step into our one precious life instead of trying to manage it.

We are not a job. We are a living, breathing human that gets to be here. We get to be! Not everyone is so lucky. Remember that perspective the next time you're in a spiral of doom. How do you want to live your one precious life? What do you actually want to focus on? Who do you want to be?

Let's reboot our lives for a future where efficiencies enabled by technology boost focus on the things that matter. It's time to radically rehaul our workplaces and relationships for the future and it's you who can help create this change by stepping into your own humanity – now, today. What will you do?

References

Introduction

Google Toolkit for Developers (no date) Digital Wellbeing, https://wellbeing.google/for-developers/ (archived at https://perma.cc/Y5VA-W2DM)

Hari, J (2023) *Stolen Focus: Why you can't pay attention*, Bloomsbury, UK

Marsden, P (2020) What is digital wellbeing? A list of definitions, digitalwellbeing.org, https://digitalwellbeing.org/what-is-digital-wellbeing-a-list-of-definitions/ (archived at https://perma.cc/9586-49E3)

Powell, G (no date) What is Digital Wellbeing? Defining a Framework to help you find it, Sentient Digital Consulting, www.sentientdigitalconsulting.com/insights/9xvyxue7djj2omogziityvtxs7krt6 (archived at https://perma.cc/GEJ6-9ZCG)

Velzeboer, P (2023) *Begin with You: Invest in your mental wellbeing and satisfaction at work*, Kogan Page

World Health Organization (2022) Mental Health, www.who.int/news-room/fact-sheets/detail/mental-health-strengthening-our-response (archived at https://perma.cc/4HLW-3AAY)

YouGov (2024) How social media has affected the mental health of Brits, https://yougov.co.uk/topics/technology/trackers/how-social-media-has-affected-the-mental-health-of-brits?period=5yrs (archived at https://perma.cc/W9NU-HLC4)

Chapter 1: Always on

Alter, A (2017) *Irresistible: The rise of addictive technology and the business of keeping us hooked*, Penguin

Brown, B (2015) *Daring Greatly: How the courage to be vulnerable transforms the way we live, love, parent, and lead*, Penguin Life

Center for Humane Technology (2021) Ledger of Harms, https://ledger.humanetech.com/ (archived at https://perma.cc/X3ST-FAVX)

Dictionary.com (no date) Grind, www.dictionary.com/browse/grind (archived at https://perma.cc/9KWV-CB6R)

Haidt, J (2024) *The Anxious Generation: How the great rewiring of childhood is causing an epidemic of mental illness*, Penguin

Hari, J (2023) *Stolen Focus: Why you can't pay attention*, Bloomsbury, UK

Harris, T (2013) A call to minimize distraction and respect users' attention, http://minimizedistraction.com/ (archived at https://perma.cc/P44C-7LXK)

Merriam-Webster Dictionary (no date) Compulsion, www.merriam-webster.com/dictionary/compulsion# (archived at https://perma.cc/3NTW-6QSG)

Orlowski, J, Coombe, D and Curtis, V (2020) *The Social Dilemma*, documentary, Netflix

University of Cambridge (2012) Rage against the machine, www.cam.ac.uk/research/news/rage-against-the-machine (archived at https://perma.cc/X857-UL2B)

Chapter 2: The psychology of digital wellbeing

Bondanini et al (2020) Technostress dark side of technology in the workplace: A scientometric analysis, *International Journal of Environmental Research and Public Health*, www.ncbi.nlm.nih.gov/pmc/articles/PMC7662498/ (archived at https://perma.cc/8Q3K-55LZ)

Brown, B (2017) *Braving the Wilderness*, Vermillion

Brunson, P (2024) *Find Love*, Vermillion

Center for Humane Technology (2021) Ledger of Harms, https://ledger.humanetech.com/ (archived at https://perma.cc/4AVY-BZTV)

Cundy, L (2018) *Attachment and the Defence Against Intimacy: Understanding and working with avoidant attachment, self-hatred, and shame*, Routledge

Dethiville, L (2018) *Donald W. Winnicott: A new approach*, Routledge

Estés, C P (2008) *Women Who Run With Wolves*, Ebury

Merriam-Webster Dictionary (no date) Potential, https://www.merriam-webster.com/dictionary/potential?utm_campaign=sd&utm_medium=serp&utm_source=jsonld (archived at https://perma.cc/72BF-TS9F)

Oxford Dictionary (no date) Potential, https://www.oed.com/dictionary/potential_adj?tab=factsheet#29047648 (archived at https://perma.cc/WAL3-BJWX)

Peterson, J (2023) https://twitter.com/jordanbpeterson/status/1726662692025278615 (archived at https://perma.cc/YM63-7S4T)

Schwarzenegger, A (2023) *Be Useful: Seven tools for life*, Penguin

Skillicorn, N (2023) It takes 23 minutes to regain focus after a distraction: Task switching, Idea to Value, www.ideatovalue.com/curi/nickskillicorn/2023/07/it-takes-23-minutes-to-regain-focus-after-a-distraction-task-switching/ (archived at https://perma.cc/C8XB-ZB68)

Walker, P (2003) Codependency, trauma and the fawn response, www.pete-walker.com/codependencyFawnResponse.htm (archived at https://perma.cc/6GC9-SP4B)

Winnicott, D W (2008) *A New Approach*, Routledge

World Health Organization (2019) Burn-out an 'occupational phenomenon': International Classification of Diseases, www.who.int/news/item/28-05-2019-burn-out-an-occupational-phenomenon-international-classification-of-diseases (archived at https://perma.cc/3BRS-KA53)

REFERENCES

Chapter 3: Comfortably numb

Aked, J, Marks, N, Cordon, C and Thompson, S (2008) Five ways to wellbeing, New Economics Foundation, https://neweconomics.org/2008/10/five-ways-to-wellbeing (archived at https://perma.cc/4NR4-MYSD)

Davies, J (2022) *Sedated: How modern capitalism created our mental health crisis*, Atlantic Books

De Botton, A (2006) *On Love*, Grove/Atlantic, Inc.

James, O (2014) *How to Develop Emotional Health*, The School of Life, Bluebird

Lewis, C S (1942) *The Screwtape Letters*, The MacMillan Company

Chapter 4: Set up to fail?

Ariely, D (2023) *Misbelief: What makes rational people believe irrational things*, Heligo Books

Center for Humane Technology (2021) Ledger of Harms, https://ledger.humanetech.com/ (archived at https://perma.cc/VT4C-LPNT)

Cole, S (2023) 'My AI is sexually harassing me': Replika users say the chatbot has gotten way too horny, *Vice*, www.vice.com/en/article/z34d43/my-ai-is-sexually-harassing-me-replika-chatbot-nudes (archived at https://perma.cc/BF2W-P38Y)

Grant, C (2022) Algorithms are making decisions about health care, which may only worsen medical racism, ACLU, www.aclu.org/news/privacy-technology/algorithms-in-health-care-may-worsen-medical-racism (archived at https://perma.cc/K3L2-WRLX)

Hari, J (2023) *Stolen Focus: Why you can't pay attention*, Bloomsbury, UK

Harris, T and Raskin, A (2023) Center for Humane Technology Co-Founders Tristan Harris and Aza Raskin discuss the AI dilemma, YouTube, www.youtube.com/watch?v=cB0_-qKbal4 (archived at https://perma.cc/J97Z-PP8N)

Hsu, T and Thompson, S (2023) Disinformation researchers raise alarms about AI chatbots, *New York Times*, www.nytimes.com/2023/02/08/technology/ai-chatbots-disinformation.html (archived at https://perma.cc/E2DW-G7QX)

Molli, V L P (2022) Effectiveness of AI-based chatbots in mental health support: A systematic review, *Journal of Healthcare AI and ML*, 9 (9), 1–11, https://journalpublication.wrcouncil.org/index.php/JHAM/article/view/10 (archived at https://perma.cc/CZ6P-PNSA)

Relate (2017) Loneliness is rising: 1 in 8 adults have no close friends, www.relate.org.uk/get-help/loneliness-rising-1-8-adults-have-no-close-friends (archived at https://perma.cc/LS4J-HT2Y)

Walker, L (2023) Belgian man dies by suicide following exchanges with chatbot, *Brussels Times*, www.brusselstimes.com/430098/belgian-man-commits-suicide-following-exchanges-with-chatgpt (archived at https://perma.cc/8URH-ULA6)

Chapter 5: Fighting loneliness and finding humanity

GilPress (2024) Loneliness Startistics Worldwide 2024, What's the Big Data, https://whatsthebigdata.com/loneliness-statistics/ (archived at https://perma.cc/83XP-AK3F)

Nelson, C A (2014) *Romania's Abandoned Children: Deprivation, brain development and the struggle for recovery*, Harvard University Press

Westcott, S (no date) How do I know if I'm lonely? UK Council for Psychotherapy, www.psychotherapy.org.uk/news/how-do-i-know-if-i-m-lonely/ (archived at https://perma.cc/WP28-32NQ)

Chapter 6: How to thrive in the digital world

Dweck, C (2012) *Mindset: How you can fulfil your potential*, Robinson
Gladwell, M (2008) *Outliers: The story of success*, Hachette
Haidt, J and Lukianoff, G (2019) *The Coddling of the American Mind*, Penguin.
Hari, J (2018) *Lost Connections: Uncovering the real causes of depression – and the unexpected solutions*, Bloomsbury, UK
Offline Club (no date) www.instagram.com/theoffline_club/ (archived at https://perma.cc/VJE6-ACQQ)
Schwarzenegger, A (2023) *Be Useful: Seven tools for life*, Penguin
Brooks, A and Winfrey, O (2023) *Build the Life You Want: The art and science of getting happier*, Penguin

Chapter 7: Create your tech boundaries

Brown, B (2018) *Dare to Lead*, Vermillion
Clear, J (2018) *Atomic Habits*, Cornerstone
Hari, J (2023) *Stolen Focus: Why you can't pay attention*, Bloomsbury, UK

Chapter 8: Find your focus and reclaim your joy

Bartlett, M, Condon, P, Cruz, J, Baumann, J and Desteno, D (2012) Gratitude: Prompting behaviours that build relationships, *Cognition and Emotion*, 26 (1), www.tandfonline.com/doi/abs/10.1080/02699931.2011.561297 (archived at https://perma.cc/6UAR-4JKF)

Csikszentmihalyi, M (1998) *Finding Flow: The psychology of engagement with everyday life*, Harper and Row

Frankl, V (1946) *Man's Search for Meaning*, Beacon Press

Perel, E (no date) www.estherperel.com/ (archived at https://perma.cc/BTF7-59EK)

Robbins, T (2022) Progress equals happiness, YouTube, https://www.youtube.com/watch?v=Z_nalShHuJY (archived at https://perma.cc/PLZ2-GF2Y)

Ware, B (2019) *The Five Regrets of the Dying*, Hay House, UK

Index

addiction
    context of 80
    distinction from compulsion 30
    risk factors for (HALT) 32
    setting boundaries 152–55
addiction to technology 3, 8, 11–12
    disconnection and anxiety caused by 111–12
    features of 28–29
    setting intentions for change 124–28
    social media 30–34
    symptoms of 58–59
advertising, emotional appeals 70
AI (artificial intelligence)
    fear of 26–27
    implications for our mental health 91–93
    use by young people 19
    use for therapy and support 93–95
Alcoholics Anonymous (AA) 59, 107, 136
Alter, Adam 31
always on, digital grind 17–36
anxiety 50
    among young people 20
    disconnection caused by tech addictions 111–12
Ariely, Dan 87
assess yourself, listen to your body 126–27
attachment, parenting and 44–45, 46–47
attachment styles
    anxious attachment 46
    assess your personal digital world 49–50
    dismissive-avoidant attachment 46
    evolving as adults 48
    fearful-avoidant attachment 46
    positive aspects of technology 48–49
    relevance to digital wellbeing 47–48
    secure attachment 46
    types of 45–46
attention
    competition for 21, 29, 53–55
    impact of smartphone usage 18–22
    inability to focus 18
authenticity 110, 184–86
autonomy, lack of 23, 25–26

belonging
    human need for 41–43, 82–84
    taking ownership of our lives 43–44
boiling frog analogy 82–84
boundaries 147–62
    accountability and support 162
    addiction and 152–55
    assess your ability to set 147–48
    coaching 162
    communicate your boundaries to those affected 160–61
    create a vision for your life 150–51
    decide what you are protecting 150–51
    digital boundaries 148–50, 157–59
    digital detox 155–57
    identify the boundaries you need 152
    practise setting a new boundary 152
    reflection prompts 161
    relational boundaries 148, 149
    setting digital boundaries 157–59
    signs that you need to set a boundary 149–50
    types of 148–49

brain fog 10
brand identity, emotional branding 71
Brooks, Arthur 121
Brown, Brene 33, 43, 74, 112, 148, 185
Brunson, Paul 45
burnout 10
    blaming the individual 7–8
    role of the environment 6–8
    technostress 50–53
busy, cult of 7–8
busyness
    as a trap 23–24
    aspect of the digital grind 23–24

CBT (cognitive behaviour therapy) 142
Center for Humane Technology 21, 42, 55, 73
    concerns about AI 92–93
    Ledger of Harms 87
change
    experimenting with 135–36
    setting intentions for 124–28
child development
    effects of early institutionalization 98–99
    how our earliest experiences shape us 61–63
    parenting and attachment 44–45, 46–47
    without technology 17–18
children, marketing to other children 84–85
Clear, James 152
clickbait 21
Coach Training Institute (CTI) 160
cognitive function, impact of technology 10–11
collective responsibility
    instead of blaming the individual 77–80
    questioning the systems around us 88–91
communication skills, developing 144
community
    building meaningful connections 137–41
    building safe spaces 142–44
    healthy vs unhealthy associations 139–41
comparison to others
    aspect of the digital grind 23, 24–25
    contribution to burnout 52
    contribution to loneliness 107
compulsion, distinction from addiction 30
connection with others
    authentic and meaningful connections 10
    be uplifting and create accountability 115–17
    check your environment 117–18
    finding opportunities for 143–44
    principles to boost connection 115–18
    ripple effect 117
    role in emotional health 67
    social skill to develop 105–06
    take brave action 115
consumerism 24
    commoditization of our emotions 69–73
    marketing wellbeing hacks 84–87
    never having enough 85
context (the machine)
    and the need to belong 82–84
    blaming the individual for struggling 77–80
    comparison with cults 79–80

how it holds us back 77–96
influence of groupthink 88–91
marketing wellbeing hacks 84–87
understanding the systemic challenges 81–82
see also environment
continuous connectivity, contribution to burnout 52
Cooke, Anne 72
cost-of-living crisis 24
Covid-19 pandemic lockdowns 105–06
crash points 10, 50–53
creating space *see* boundaries
creativity, impact of being in survival mode 42–43
critical thinking 142
Csikszentmihalyi, Mihaly 171–73
cult life
　and the need to belong 82–84
　blaming the individual 77
　boiling frog analogy 82–84
　effects of growing up in a cult 7–8
　what it can tell us about the machine 79–80
Cundy, Lindy 47–48

data privacy issues 21
Davies, James 69–70, 72
de Botton, Alain 61
depression 50
　among young people 20
digital boundaries *see* boundaries
digital burnout 50–53
digital detox 3–4, 80–82, 155–57
digital education, need for 29
digital grind
　always-on culture 17–36
　busyness aspect 23–24
　constant comparing to others 23, 24–25
　distraction aspect 23–24
　evolving into a fulfilling future 35–36
　lack of autonomy 23, 25–26
　recognising your digital grind 34–35
　side-hustles 23, 24–25
　what it feels like 22–26
digital malaise 57–76
　challenging by embracing our humanity 61
　challenging the thinking that easier is better 63–69
　commoditization of emotions 69–73
　dissociation 62–63, 64–65
　experiencing and acknowledging our emotions 73–75
　foundations for emotional health 66–69
　how our devices are keeping us stuck 60–61
　how our earliest experiences shape us 61–63
　how to challenge it 73–75
　response to painful emotions 57–58
　symptoms of digital addiction 58–59
digital overwhelm 10–11, 27–28
digital wellbeing
　assess your digital and wellbeing practices 113–15
　assess your personal digital world 49–50
　authentic and meaningful connections 10
　cognitive function and focus 10–11
　definitions of 8–11
　everyday challenges 181–83
　Five Ways to Wellbeing 66–67
　mental health 9–10, 11–12

digital wellbeing (*Continued*)
  physical health 9
  psychology of 37–56
  relevance of attachment styles 47–48
  skills for 183–86
disconnection
  caused by addiction to technology 111–12
  digital polarization of views 112
  effects of smartphones 97–98
  human need for connection with others 98–99
Dispenza, Joe 101, 163
dissociation 62–63, 64–65
distractions
  aspect of the digital grind 23–24
  contribution to burnout 52
  sleep disruption caused by 53
dopamine 28, 61
  addiction and 30
  effects of physical activity 66
Dweck, Carol 132

Einstein, Albert 102
emotional dependency on digital products 71
emotional health, foundations for 66–69
emotionally charged advertising 70
emotions
  commoditization of 69–73
  experiencing and acknowledging 73–75
empathy 184
environment
  impact on wellbeing 117–18
  influence on mental health 6–8
  systemic problems that make us sick 12–13
  see also context (the machine)

environmental toxicity, blaming the individual for struggling 77–80
Estés, Clarissa 44
ethical issues related to technology 20–21
experiential marketing 71

failure, how the context/environment holds us back 77–80
fake news 21
fawn response to social stress 40
fear
  of missing out 52
  of progress and technology 26–27
feedback on your relationship to technology 129–30
feeling better, taking ownership of our lives 43–44
feelings, information from 141–42
fight, flight, freeze or fawn responses to stress 40
Five Ways to Wellbeing 66–67
five-year plans 151
fixed mindset 132
flow state 171–73
focus
  enabling joy 164
  flow state 171–73
  impact of smartphone usage 18–22
  impact of technology 10–11
  inability to pay attention 18
  managing distractions 171–73
  progress, not perfection 176–79
  The Five Regrets of the Dying 175–76
  tough love 173–76
  what good looks like 123–24
Frankl, Victor 165
freeze response to toxic stress 40

INDEX

Gandhi 136
Gardner, Chris 177–78
Gen Z 19, 174–75
giving back 66–67, 170–71
Gladwell, Malcolm 133
Goggins, David 173
Google 11, 21, 82
gratitude practice 165–66
groupthink 88–90, 140
    questioning how we relate to others 90–91
growth mindset 132–33, 157, 165, 167
gut instinct 140–41

habits, creating new ones 152
Haidt, Jonathan 20, 141–42
HALT (risk factors for addiction) 32
Hari, Johann 12, 18, 81, 137, 138, 155
Harris, Tristan 21, 92
hatred of others 65, 69
Heraclitus 135
humanity
    embracing who we are 185–86
    making true connections 111–13
hypervigilance 52

imposter syndrome 107
Industrial Revolution 26
information overload
    contribution to burnout 52
    wellbeing hacks 85–86
innovation, impact of being in survival mode 42–43
intentions
    definition of an intention 125–26
    how to listen to your body 126–27
    how to set an intention 127–28
    setting intentions for change 124–28

Jackson, Kat Cormack 48
James, Oliver 62–63
Jobs, Steve 84
joy 74
    action steps 179
    approach to reclaiming 163–64
    cultivate a positive mindset 169–70
    engage in activities you love 166
    foster healthy relationships 167
    give back 170–71
    how to cultivate it 164–71
    limit negative influences 169–70
    mindfulness and meditation 168–69
    practise gratitude 165–66
    practise kindness 170–71
    progress, not perfection 176–79
    take care of your physical health 167
    The Five Regrets of the Dying 175–76
    tough love 173–76

kindness, acts of 170–71

learning
    cultivating your potential 38–39
    role in emotional health 67
Lembke, Ann 30
Lewis, CS 65
listen to your body 126–27
loneliness 97–119
    assess your digital and wellbeing practices 113–15
    boosting humanity and making true connections 111–13
    causes of 100

loneliness (*Continued*)
  creating change in a lonely society 118–19
  digital loneliness 111
  feeling of shame associated with 104, 107–09
  how it shapes us 104–05
  imposter syndrome 107
  letting go and embracing change 110–11
  paradox of internal isolation 104–05
  principles to boost connection 115–18
  rates of 99–100
  recognizing unhealthy loneliness 113
  remote working 101–03
  signs and symptoms of 100–01
  stigma and taboo associated with 107–09
  taking responsibility for our wellbeing 109–11
Luddites 26
Lukianoff, Greg 141–42

machine *see* context
marketing
  emotion data mining 70
  emotionally engaging experiences 71
  manipulating emotional responses 71–72
  neuromarketing 71–72
Marsden, Paul 8–9
Maslow's hierarchy of needs 63–64
meaning in your life 143
meditation 67, 168–69
meeting culture, inefficiencies of 89–90
Mehran, Ardeshir 138–39
mental health
  aspect of digital wellbeing 9–10
  challenges for young people 20–22
  definitions of 11
  digital burnout 50–53
  impact of smartphone use 18–22
  impact of your technology 4–6
  implications of AI 91–93
  influence of toxic environments 6–8
  relationship to digital health 11–12
  systemic challenges 53–55
  systems that commoditize our emotions 69–73
  use of AI for therapies and support 93–95
  what good looks like 122–23
mental toughness 173–76
mind-wandering 18, 164
mindfulness 67, 167–68
mindset
  fixed mindset 132
  growth mindset 132–33, 157, 165, 167
  reflection as a mindset 183
  victim mindset 110, 165
misinformation 21
  susceptibility to 87–88
multitasking, contribution to burnout 52

negativity bias 42–43
Nelson, Charles A 98–99
neuromarketing 71–72
Nike 70–71
notifications and alerts, triggering survival responses 41

overwhelm *see* digital overwhelm

parenting, development of child attachment styles 44–45, 46–47

Perel, Esther 167
personal responsibility, taking ownership of our lives 43–44
perspective on life 170
Peterson, Jordan 38
physical activity, role in emotional health 66
physical health
   aspect of digital wellbeing 9
   taking care of 167
polarization of views, influence of algorithms 112
political division 21
pornography 10
positive mindset 169–70
   toxic positivity 116–17
potential
   cultivating through learning 38–39
   definition of 38
   impact of being in survival mode 42–43
   impact of lack of autonomy 25–26
   loss in digital distractions 33–34
   mental health and 11
   what stops us reaching our potential 39–40
   why it matters 37–39
Powell, Georgie 11
presence, living in the here and now 183
privacy issues 21
product placement 84
psychology of digital wellbeing 37–56

quantum energy and remote working 101–03

Raskin, Aza 92

reflection, as a habit and a mindset 183
relational boundaries 148, 149
relationships
   foster healthy relationships 167
   questioning how we relate to others 90–91
remote working, building connections 101–03
resentment, sign that you need to set a boundary 149
resilience 49–50, 74, 140, 174–75, 183–84
Robbins, Tony 176–77
Romanian orphanage children 98–99
Roosevelt, Theodore 185

safe spaces, building 142–44
Schwarzenegger, Arnold 38, 143, 151, 173
self-awareness 62–63, 65
self-harm, rates among young people 20
self-identity 62–63
shame
   associated with feeling lonely 104, 107–09
   digital addiction and 32–33
side-hustles 23, 24–25
skills
   for digital wellbeing 183–86
   for engaging in the adult world 49–50
   nurturing connections 105–06
   social skills 105–06
sleep disruption, caused by digital distractions 53
smartphones
   disconnection from others 97–98
   history and impact of 18–22
Smith, Will 178

snowflake generation 173–75
social media
  addiction to 30–34
  contribution to burnout 52
  engagement through emotional content 70–71
  negativity bias 42–43
stigma and taboo, associated with feeling lonely 107–09
stress
  digital overwhelm 27–28
  fight, flight, freeze or fawn responses 40
  unhealthy coping mechanisms 87–88
suicide, rates among young people 20
survival mode
  being stuck in 39–40
  human need for belonging 41–43
  impact on creativity and innovation 42–43
  negativity bias 42–43
  search for certainty 65
survival responses
  fight, flight, freeze or fawn 40
  triggered by devices 41
systemic challenges to our mental health 12–13, 53–55

technology
  addiction to *see* addiction to technology
  as a kind of psychic retreat 47–48
  fear of 26–27
  impact on mental health 4–6
  positive aspects of connection with likeminded people 48–49
  reflecting on your relationship with 1–4

systemic challenges to our mental health 53–55
triggering survival responses 41
technophobia 26–27
technostress 8, 50–53
TED talks 21
The Pursuit of Happyness (movie) 177–78
The Social Dilemma (Netflix documentary) 19–20, 30
Thomas, Eric (The Hip Hop Preacher) 173–74
thriving in the digital world 121–45
  approach to 121–22
  building community and meaningful connections 137–41
  building safe spaces 142–44
  experimenting with change 135–36
  feedback on your relationship with technology 129–30
  grassroots solutions 130–32
  information from your feelings 141–42
  setting intentions for change 124–28
  taking responsibility for ourselves 136
  things that can help us thrive 132–36
  what good looks like 122–24
Time Well Spent movement 21
toxic positivity 116–17

victim mindset 110, 165
vision or goal for your life 142–43, 150–51
volunteering 170

Ware, Bonnie 175–76

wellbeing
    taking responsibility for 109–11
    tough love 173–76
    see also digital wellbeing
wellbeing hacks, selling solutions to problems created by the system 84–87
Westcott, Stephen 100–01
Winfrey, Oprah 121
Winnicott, Donald 45
work, what good looks like 123–24

workplace
    impact of lack of autonomy 23, 25–26
    impact on wellbeing 117–18
    inefficiencies of meeting culture 89–90
    influence of groupthink 89–90

young people, mental health challenges 20–22
YouTube, motivation videos 173–74

Looking for another book?

Explore our award-winning books from global business experts in General Business

Scan the code to browse

www.koganpage.com/general-business

More from Kogan Page

ISBN: 9781398610316

ISBN: 9781398613911

ISBN: 9781398616103

ISBN: 9781398617360

www.koganpage.com